APOCALYPSE LATER

ZINE
ISSUE #2

"That remains my favourite review anyone did of it, just because you grokked so much of what I was going for."

— Jasper DeWitt on *The Patient*

APOCALYPSE LATER BOOKS
BY HAL C. F. ASTELL

FILM

Huh? An A-Z of Why Classic American Bad Movies Were Made
Velvet Glove Cast in Iron: The Films of Tura Satana
Charlie Chaplin Centennial: Keystone
The International Horror & Sci-Fi Film Festival: The Transition Years
A Hundred in 2016
The Awesomely Awful '80s, Part 2
A Horror Movie Calendar

ZINE

Horns Ablaze #1
The Library of Halexandria #1

APOCALYPSE LATER ZINE #2

The Library of Halexandria #1

REVIEWS FROM THE NAMELESS ZINE
NEW INTERVIEWS

ARIZONA AUTHORS #1

APOCALYPSE LATER PRESS
PHOENIX, AZ

Apocalypse Later Zine #002 — November 2022

The Library of Halexandria #1: Arizona Authors #1

ISBN-13: 978-1-961279-08-7

Apocalypse Later Press catalogue number: ALZ002

Some of this material was originally published online at the Nameless Zine.

https://thenamesszine.org

Cover art generated at Wombo.

https://dream.ai/

Apocalypse Later is a monthly zine published by Apocalypse Later Press. Each third issue is a *Library of Halexandria* edition, covering a themed set of book reviews and adding interviews as applicable.

Typeset in Cantarell, Gentium Plus, Linux Biolinum, Oswald ExtraLight, Twlg Typist and Veteran Typewriter.

https://fonts.adobe.com/fonts/cantarell

https://software.sil.org/gentium/

https://sourceforge.net/projects/linuxlibertine/

https://fonts.adobe.com/fonts/oswald

https://packages.debian.org/buster/fonts-tlwg-typist-ttf

https://liveheroes.com/en/brand/typesgal

Published through Kindle Direct Publishing

https://kdp.amazon.com/

Published by Apocalypse Later Press

https://press.apocalypselaterempire.com/

DEDICATION

To every Arizona author, past, present and future. A rising tide floats all boats.

CONTENTS

GRATUITOUS BLANK PAGE FOR ME TO GET A BUNCH OF AUTOGRAPHS

INTRODUCTION

I wasn't born in Arizona but I've lived here for almost twenty years and, for almost all of that time, I've been writing. By one standard, that makes me an Arizona writer, and, once I got some books into print, I became an Arizona author.

I had met a number of authors back in the U.K. and had become involved at points with writing and publishing, but it wasn't a core thing for me. Most obviously, I did some work with Guy N. Smith, laying out a few issues of his fan club magazine, *Graveyard Rendezvous*, and also a couple of his books and chapbooks. I had experience there through editing my local parish magazine and starting up a self-funded magazine covering my village of Barkisland.

I'd written quite a bit too, but nothing much publishable. I'd had a few short stories published and I was earning money for the electric meter writing custom poems for people. I'd also started to take Jerry Pournelle's advice to wannabe writers and wrote a series of daily pieces that were aimed at getting me to the million words it takes to become a writer. I eventually published those as *The Million Word March*, because it worked, albeit maybe not quite that quickly.

Most of my writing came here in Arizona, to which I moved in 2004. That's when I started up a blog that lasted, wrote and published actual books and started to appear at events so I could try to persuade the public to hand over their hard earned cash for something with my name on it. I've never become a bestseller but I have become an award-winner and I've learned a heck of a lot here in the Arizona writing community.

In doing so, I've got to know a lot of Arizona authors who have either sold me copies of their books or agreed to swap them for mine, and it seemed logical to review some of those once I had been brought on board the Nameless Zine as a staff writer. However, it was the untimely death of Alan Black that prompted me to do that on an organised basis.

I'd sold books alongside Alan at a number of events, especially Phoenix Comicons, and he was the single author who taught me more than anyone else. I've benefitted substantially from his advice. I'd bought a few of his books that he kindly signed for me, but I hadn't read any of them before he passed and that felt wrong. So I read and reviewed all his science fiction books and found that, as well as being a damn good human being, he was also a damn good writer.

So are many other Arizona authors, some of them friends, some acquaintances, some people I haven't even met yet, and I started to shine an organised light on their work by reviewing at least one Arizona book each month at the Nameless Zine, starting in September 2020. This zine collects a bunch of earlier reviews of books written by Arizona authors and everything from that point on. There will be future volumes down the road.

Note: some are Arizona authors in the same way I am. Jeff Mariotte moved in. Beth Cato and David Riley moved in and out again. David Lee Summers works here. Suyi Davies Okungbowa studied here. John Paul Ried, Tom Leveen and Sara Fujimura are all elsewhere now. But I think of them all as fellow Arizona authors, part of a vibrant writing community. Check out their work!

INTERVIEW

DANI HOOTS

AL: How early in life did you start reading and who did you read as a child?

DH: I can't remember that far back to be honest. I remember reading *The Happy Hollisters* when I was really young... and then I got into reading *Star Wars Legends* books and lots of Asimov.

AL: What's the first thing you remember writing and how awful was it, looking back from now?

DH: I used to write fanfics where I was a Sailor Scout and fought bad guys in *Sailor Moon*. I think they might be in a box somewhere. They were pretty bad, but I was in elementary school so they weren't *that* bad for how old I was.

AL: When do you feel like you figured writing out and what was the key to getting to that point?

DH: I don't think any of us are at that point. The more practice you get in, the more you learn. I feel like I'm always learning new things, whether it be creatively or for marketing.

AL: You're unusually prolific. What's your writing routine and how did COVID-19 work for you?

DH: I don't really have a routine per se, but I wrote most of my books during COVID-19 since I have an autoimmune disorder and was stuck inside for months... upon months... I want to start dictating my novels, though, as I commute to school. I tested it out and got some foundation for three chapters in one day. I'm hoping it will streamline the process since I haven't written much in the past year.

AL: You started out with unusual vampires but write in many genres. Which genre is home and why?

DH: I actually started out with sci-fi. *A World of Vampires* were a close second, but my first book published was *A Falling Starr*, of which was published 10 years ago (I just celebrated my 10 year publishing anniversary!). So I would have to say sci-fi since I grew up reading and writing it. The first book I finished writing (*The Quest*) was sci-fi as well.

AL: You seem well read in culture, history, language, myth... do you seek ideas or do they seek you?

DH: They seek me. They will pop up in my head and take over. I have a whiteboard with a list of all my ideas, and there are 25 or so different series ideas on it.

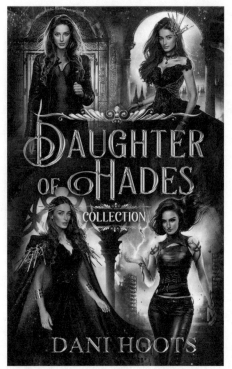

AL: With so much YA urban fantasy on TV, which of your series would translate best to that medium?

DH: I think of all my fantasy series, *Daughter of Hades* would do best as a show. People like mythology and it's set in modern day London mostly.

AL: Which of your books are you most fond of and why? And which is the best one to start with?

DH: I'm most fond of *The Quest*—mainly because it was the first one I wrote so it feels like home. Most people start out with my *Daughter of Hades* series though, it just depends what genre you like.

AL: What are your favourite books of the last five years, not including your own?

DH: I really enjoyed *Daughter of Sparta* by Claire M. Andrews, *Echo North* by Joanna Ruth Meyer, *Gunslinger Girl* by Lyndsay Ely, and *Death of the Dawn* by Amanda V. King.

AL: And finally, name one other Arizona author that people should absolutely check out.

DH: I recommend Sonja F. Blanco! She writes amazing YA witch fantasy. She just finished her *Witch of Warewoods* trilogy that you all should check out!

danihoots.com
facebook.com/danihootsauthor
instagram.com/danihootsauthor
pinterest.com/danihootsauthor
twitter.com/danihootsauthor

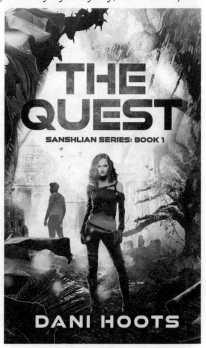

INTERVIEW
S. C. MENDES

AL: How early in life did you start reading and who did you read as a child?

SCM: I was fortunate to begin reading at an early age. Like most '80s kids, I participated in Scholastic fairs at school. My genre of choice was mystery. Often, they were dark mysteries or contained a supernatural slant, something in the vein of *Fear Street* or *Goosebumps*. Around middle school, I fell in love with *The Twilight Zone* TV show. This led to the discovery of author Richard Matheson, and he was my bridge from YA fiction to more adult short stories and eventually novels. *I Am Legend* still holds a special place in my heart, and I stand by the claim that no film adaptation has gotten it right yet.

AL: What's the first thing you remember writing and how awful was it, looking back from now?

SCM: That's a toss up between *Ninja* and an untitled manuscript which was really just a rip-off of *The Lord of the Rings*. Not that *Ninja* was much better; it was basically a retelling of the Michael Dudikoff movie *American Ninja* mixed with dark fantasy elements. Both stories were epically awful. Perhaps a twelve-year-old can be forgiven, though.

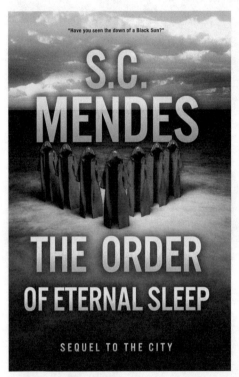

AL: When do you feel like you figured writing out and what was the key to getting to that point?

SCM: Every time I think I've got writing figured out, it slips through my grasp. The current aspect of writing I'm exploring is perception. It's fascinating how two people can read the same piece of literature and yet walk away with vastly different interpretations.

In my own writing, I experiment with perception by measuring how much character motivation I clarify versus how much is left ambiguous, then observing how that satisfies readers or not. I'm fascinated to see how people receive and interpret a book based on what I choose to reveal or conceal. This isn't to say, I obsess over reader interpretations. But I try to let it inform me when I approach future manuscripts. I ask myself what the purpose of the book is, who is the audience and what's the most effective POV for them.

This doesn't always make your writing popular; though it gets the message to the right readers. It's often the reason why your favorite authors always have one or two books you just don't understand what they were thinking when they wrote it. You see this with music albums and other forms of art. There's always experimental projects that cause a rift among fans as to its worthiness.

AL: What sparked *The City*? Worldbuilding isn't one of horror's strong suits, but you nailed that.

SCM: A few years back, I asked myself that same question. I get a lot of love from David Icke fans, who assume the idea came from him. But I honestly had no idea of his reptilian agenda in 2007 when I first wrote the short story that would become *The City*.

I discovered that the inspiration began as a child playing in my dad's library. He had a bunch of strange fantasy books, which I've been come the keeper of now. And most of which I never read. Not even now that I'm older. The covers however left impressions on me, and for years, I daydreamed of what the stories might have been about.

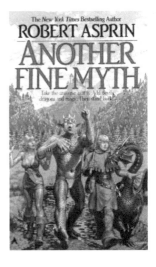

Inspiration for the Mara specifically came from the *Myth Inc.* series by Robert Asprin. They were a race of interdimensional

demons, but that's all I remember.

AL: There's both Sax Rohmer and Clive Barker in *The City*. How did you merge those different eras?

SCM: The idea of mingling detectives of *Fu Manchu*-era crime and Clive Barker-esque demons came from staring at those wild fantasy covers from the '80s, and my childhood love of mystery. Books from Craig Shaw Gardner's *Cineverse Cycle* series always had humans and detectives pitted alongside monsters and fantasy beings.

Instead of an interdimensional portal to cenobites, The City was a physical location, a place you could find and access. A place that wasn't really "magical," but perhaps more the physical manifestation of the spiritual hell where Pinhead resides. The creatures of The City incorporate an occult/spiritual science, although, only toward the end of the second book is the science of the Mara explored in more depth. The third book goes into greater detail how these beings came to exist as well as the Ming's years working for Shin Sho.

AL: How do you find time to write, given that you also run a very active small press, Blood Bound Books?

SCM: And teach part time.

The short answer is "I don't find much time." Haha. The biggest obstacle in my personal writing is definitely Blood Bound Books. And yet the press brings me some of the greatest joy in my life. Being able to meet authors from around the world and contribute to bringing their books to life is an amazing feeling.

As such, I have come to terms with taking a while between book releases. I hope my readers can understand and check out all Blood Bound Books' titles while they wait for my next one.

AL: You write collaboratively with Nikki Noir. How is that process better and worse than writing solo?

SCM: With short stories, one of us usually writes the primary idea and pitches a rough

outline with places highlighted where we think the other person may shine. For example, in our newest book *Corrosive Ravens*, I suggested a scene where the POV is a female virgin arguing about sex with her boyfriend for the first time. I suggested Nikki write that scene as I think a female author may bring a more accurate pers-pective for that character.

The con is you're beholden to someone else. But that's also the benefit.

If you're ready to write one morning and you've got time, but your co-author hasn't completed their part yet, then you have to wait. It cultivates patience. By the same token, it gives you much more immediate feedback. Often a writer won't receive a strong critique until a work is completed and goes to a beta reader. Correcting plot issues at this stage can be time consuming. However, you can catch flaws so much quicker when you co-write.

It's cool getting to read a scene in your book written by someone else. Goes back to changing that perspective. Co-authoring is something I think every writer should do at least once in their career, even if just with a short story, just to have the experience.

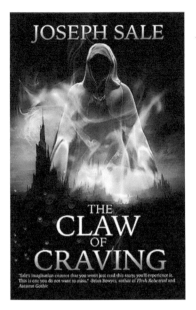

AL: What's the next big idea from S. C. Mendes once you wrap up the City trilogy?

SCM: *Suck-U-Bus* was so well received, Nikki and I have decided to finish that story. The seed was planted in *Suck-U-Bus*, and readers seem to want to know why Tonya double-crossed Lisa and who Dominic is. So we've already started *Corrosive Ravens*. It is the prequel, and the origin of Tonya and The Mothers. It will be fun heavy metal, B-movie horror.

AL What are your favourite books of the last five years, not including your own?

SCM: *The Lost Carcosa* series by Joseph Sale has gotten me back into fantasy. After middle school and my failed attempt at ripping off *The Lord of the Rings*, I slowly lost interest with most subgenres of fantasy. Eventually, I did this for more than a decade. But taking a chance on Sale's series made epic fantasy fun again.

AL: And finally, name one other Arizona author that people should absolutely check out.

SMC: Check out Yvonne Navarro.

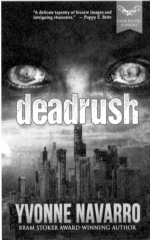

bloodgutsandstory.com
facebook.com/mendeshorror/
bloodboundbooks.etsy.com

INTERVIEW
ERNEST HOGAN

How early in life did you start reading and who did you read as a child?

In early grade school I actually had a hard time learning to read. I'm dyslexic, but back then they would just tell you that you're lazy and have to try harder. Spend a lot of time at the table with the other kids who the teacher had given up on—do they still do that?

Then I discovered comic books. It does make a difference when you're interested in what you're reading. I still find kid lit boring. Soon I was reading faster and at a higher level than my classmates, but kept it secret when a teacher screamed at someone, "There's no way you're read that far already!" I was a lot farther. Me and school never got along so good.

What's the first thing you remember writing and how awful was it, looking back from now?

About 1970, when I was starting high school, I wrote a letter to a comic book and when they published it, I got into print at age 13. It changed my life. For a few years, I wrote a lot of letters of comment that were printed in various comic books. I'm terrified of looking at them.

When do you feel like you figured writing out and what was the key to getting to that point?

It happens to me now and then, but luckily, I keep coming to my senses. I'm still figuring it out. I kept changing my mind about how to do it. The more you write, the more you learn. I have decades of experience, and hesitate about giving advice—unless I'm getting paid, and in that case, I at least try to be entertaining.

What's it like being the father of an entire genre? Has that helped or hindered your career?

The Father of Chicano Science Fiction thing started out as a joke. I like to say that I deserve something for my years of humping the Unholy Genre, and point out that there hasn't been a DNA test. In the year 2000 I thought my career was over, now I'm a weird influence. There are people who wish they had a career like mine. I'm not sure what genre I'm writing or creating. I'm just a Chicanonaut exploring a strange universe, and my work is the result of my interactions, like the wreckage left behind after a giant monster stomps through town. I'm a legend in the literary barrio, but New York is still debating as to whether or not I actually exist.

Talking of genre, what genre do you consider you write, given that it seems to be many all at once?

I've published in a lot of venues that have "science fiction" as part of their names. Realism is never enough for me. Sur-? Magical? I prefer scientific explanations and hablo fluent sci-fi, so it all comes out that way, even what I'm just being far-out. I get congratulated that my straight reporting is so imaginative. I tend to just do what I do and leave it to others to hang labels on me. Did I mention that I am not now, nor have I ever been a card-carrying cyberpunk? Gonzo? Sure, why not?

You blur languages. Which do you write in and which do you think in? Does it shape your work?

Like I keep saying, I was born in East L.A. and my mother's maiden name is Garcia. My toddler years were pure Spanglish. I wasn't aware that there were two separate languages until we moved to West Covina, and I started going to school with the pale people from "Backeast" and even the teachers didn't know what a tortilla was. My Chicano background makes me irreverent to English, which is actually a hot raquache/meztijae mess of languages from empires collided over the ages. I love a good multilingual trainwreck, and put them in my work.

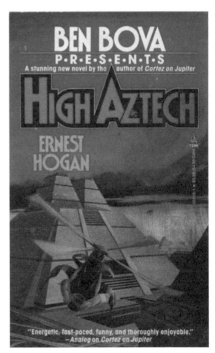

Your novels are utterly unlike anyone else's. How important is it to have your own unique voice?

People do tend to remember my work, and that probably helps. I can't seem to help being unique. I get bored when I have to do things the way everyone does, or have to do something over and over. I often try doing this in a new way, just to see what happens. Of course, it means I'm not considered commercial, and what I do can be considered in bad taste and incorrect, politically and otherwise. I suppose if there was more really weird shit out there to read, I wouldn't need write so much of it.

Each of your novels screams cult movie, should someone get it right. Or are you too wild for film?

Uh-oh—this puts me in danger of going off on a wild tangent about my near-misses—like a pass in a bullfight where the torero gets blood in his shirt— with l'art du cinema... I gave up my dreams of being a filmmaker when I realized that I'm not a people-wrangler and don't have the gift of being able to talk folks into giving large amounts of money. At least when you write something you can get it the way you want it, at least until you hear back from an editor. I've had inquiries about a the rights to all my novels... and I'm not holding my breath. My short story *The Frankenstein Penis* [collected in *Guerrilla Mural of a Siren's Song*] has been made into at least two student films, and had then a guy who makes commercials got in touch, then ghosted me. I've been told I should get an agent...

What are your favourite books of the last five years, not including your own?

Fear and Loathing in Las Vegas - Hunter S. Thompson
Black Empire - George S. Schuyler
Jamaica Ginger - Nalo Hopkinson
Goddess of Filth - V. Castro
The Daughter of Doctor Moreau - Silvia Moreno-Garcia
Mayan Calendar Girls - Team 2012

Team 2012 is Cammy May Hunnicutt, Linton Robinson, Grayson Moran and others.

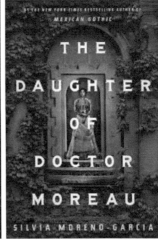

And finally, name one other Arizona author that people should absolutely check out.

Hey, everybody! Read my wife's books! She's published as Emily Devenport, Lee Hogan, and Maggy Thomas. She constantly surprises me. Probably why I married her.

mondoernesto.com
facebook.com/ernest.hogan/
twitter.com/NestoHogan

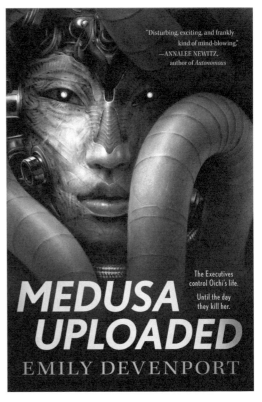

INTERVIEW

MONA VENTRESS

How early in life did you start reading and who did you read as a child?

I was an early and voracious reader. My parents got me hooked on phonics when I was a kid, and then my mom and dad would read to me all the time, but would start to get 'busy' around the end of the book, forcing me to finish reading it on my own. The first book I remember doing this with was *Dragonriders of Pern* (omitting some of the sexier parts, which I totally went back and read—but that's a different story), and after that, I was hooked on the written word.

I was always hooked on fantasy, but Robert Jordan was my favorite through and through. I must've worn out/destroyed three hardback copies of *The Eye of the World* because I read them so many times. I just remember the women being

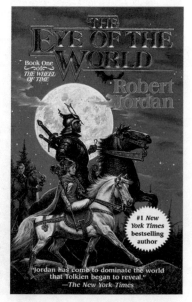

powerful and that was so different from the other books I'd read in the series.

Oh, and Piers Anthony's *Xanth* novels, but those are so much harder to read now; the sexism is strong with those ones.

What's the first thing you remember writing and how awful was it, looking back from now?

Excluding the book I created as a kindergarten project about an ant named Anthony who got lost and needed to find his way home, the first really cringe/formative writing I completed was when I was 16 and really into fast cars. I wrote a Mad Max-esque story about a group of teens being funded by the CIA to defend what was the remnants of the Western United States after a nuke had taken it out. It was a hot mess, featuring a main character named Janet who was pregnant, didn't want to be, and wound up dying half-way through the book with the order to come get me (yes, ME— I wrote myself into the story in true Mary Sue fashion) to save the day. *Sigh* It was so so SO bad, and yet I REALLY regret not having a copy to look back on and see how much I've grown.

When do you feel like you figured writing out and what was the key to getting to that point?

I think I just got tired of not reading the things I wanted to read. I'd get so angry seeing the heroes and/or heroines have the same tropes, the same foibles, the same miscommunications over and over and over again, and hated it. I wanted to see real people doing things, facing their traumas, and getting better! Not the same regurgitated toxic B.S. Not that toxic B.S. can't be fun... but, for me,

books were the tools that helped me identify positive and negative traits in people as the writers understood them, and I want to contribute an elevated version of that, one that deepens our understanding of humanity based on my own perceptions.

So, mythological smut... how did that idea come about? And how quickly did it take form?

I mean, who hasn't wanted to shag a god? I was always hot for Cernunnos, especially when I learned he had a schlong as tall as his chin. And then there were the maiden sacrifices to the minotaur? HOT, with a capital hubba-hubba-hubba. And it's not like I'm the only one out there; people have been writing sex stories about gods and other mythological beings for centuries.

The true catalyst for behind the whole project was when an author got overnight infamy for

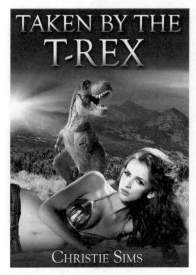

writing dinosaur erotica. Christie Sims, the author of *Taken by the T-Rex*, somehow managed to take the internet briefly by storm in 2013 and—despite receiving a middling star rating—shot up to the top of Amazon's erotica best sellers list by the sheer volume of curious people needing to understand just how this human woman was 'taken' by a T-Rex.

It's short, well-paced, and every bit as bad (yet somehow good?) as you're thinking, and yes—it absolutely inspired me to go for it and put those mythological fantasies onto paper. Once the decision was made, the only thing left was the how. How to approach it. How to make it stand out. How to make it different than what traditional erotica did before. The A-Z idea was one of many to emerge at that time, and my love of alliteration sealed the deal to commit to that, especially the more I talked about it with my friends. (Sidebar: I think one of the biggest disappointments was that Christy Sims's other book titles weren't as alliterative as the T-Rex one, but I made sure to rectify that in my series).

All in all, it took anywhere from 3 to 5 years before I had fully visualized what the series should be, plus another 2 to 3 years that I took to write, shred, rewrite, set on fire, and then eventually re-rewrite it into what I knew it could be. Is it perfect? No. But it's mine, and I love it. I just hope others love it too.

With your A-Z approach, which letter are you looking forward to the most and least?

Spoiler alert, lol!

Most of the series is flexible, but there are a few "fixed points in time", to quote the Doctor, that I'm both looking forward to and dreading. I'll start with the elephant in the room, "H". As my readers well know, I've been slowly building toward something happening with Hermes, and let me tell you —it is a doozy. I don't think my brain has let me get past that point yet, but when I get there, I'll definitely update my answer.

26 novellas (or novels) is a huge commitment. Are you writing any-thing else on the side?

God, I wish! I have so many plans—so many stories brewing in my diabolical imagination—and it blows that I can't telepathically will them onto paper instead of manually typing them out. My goal is to do my writing full-time, but until my books are doing well enough to cover the cost of existing, I'll have to eat my literary elephant one small bite at a time.

How crucial is balancing the smut with humour, character and back story, both human and god?

As essential as breathing! Sex is extremely personal, but when it's shared with someone it exposes you to the whole range of human emotion. Guilt, pleasure, shame, joy, confusion, and yes, of course, humor—all informed by a person's character and experiences!

While yes, I realize we're talking about characters, at the end of the day, characters ARE people, and the more real we—as authors—make them, the more readers can connect with them. I want readers to know that those awkward experiences aren't held by them alone. Write things that have them empathizing with a character when they're feeling shame or guilty. And, of course, they should enjoy all the parts that leave their tummies squirming and lungs panting for more.

How do you market mythological smut and what audiences have you found that you didn't expect?

I don't have much of a marketing plan—I target audiences that already enjoy monster-fucking themes, namely women who are so-fed up with real-life monsters that they have to seek solace with the fantasy ones just to feel safe. However, I have been surprised to find that a lot of couples enjoy reading my smut to each other, and honestly, I am here for it! It's such a great demonstration of how healthy that couple's sex life is, and I want to see so much more of that. I do wish more men would buy them to read them—erotica written by women could give them such insight into the inner workings of the female mind—but I have hope they will come around soon.

What are your favourite books of the last five years, not including your own?

So, full confession—reading has been REALLY hard for me the past few years. So much of my work involves the written word (not just writing books but putting together instruction guides and other documents for my job), and I used to be a ghost writer, so it's very easy for me to glom on to other styles that it's difficult to shake off when I want to use my natural voice. As such, I haven't been reading as much as I used to or would like. I guess that means my books are my favourite books of the last five years??

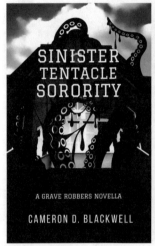  

And finally, name one other Arizona author that people should absolutely check out.

Oh man, great question! I'm not sure I can limit it to one, but I will whittle it down to two! Cameron Blackwell is first – he writes fantastic queer sci-fi and fantasy adventures, and even has a series set in modern-day Tucson. Then there's James Sabata – he writes phenomenal horror and will raise money for charity through Go Fund Me, allowing his fans to become characters who die in his next book! I can't wait for his next one; I'm definitely going to sign-up to get killed-off in a most gruesome and gory fashion!

wordsmithindustries.llc/author-mona-ventress
facebook.com/profile.php?id=100079085808419
instagram.com/monaventressauthor/
tiktok.com/@mona_ventress
x.com/ventressmona

INTERVIEW

JOHN PAUL RIED

How early in life did you start reading and who did you read as a child?

I was born with seven major birth defects resulting from fetal alcohol syndrome. Nineteen years of physical therapy on my legs, repeated eye surgeries, and other issues kept me reading and enjoying books as a boy. I read everything given to me.

Three authors were my favorites growing up. JRR Tolkien's *The Hobbit*, *The Lord of the Rings*, even *The Silmarillion* was a major influence. James Clavell's Asian saga and especially *Shogun* was another crucial favorite of mine. Finally Isaac Asimov, who was a close, personal friend of my grandfather Darrell Blaine Lucas who raised me, with his *Robot*, *Empire* and *Foundation* books, always made me smile, These three authors greatly influenced my own writings.

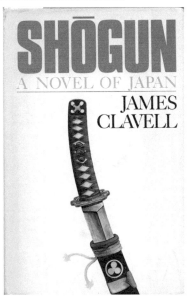

What's the first thing you remember writing and how awful was it, looking back from now?

I once wrote *John Plays Army Man*, in 2nd grade. Of course, I blew up the city of Moscow with the evil Godless Commies and the USA unified the planet with feeding everyone. Have I changed? I hope so and hope not.

When do you feel like you figured writing out and what was the key to getting to that point?

In 2012, I was running a D&D game for friends when one of my players discovered all the files I had about my campaign home world of Palamar. Her name was Laura Thompson and she read a short story I typed up and loved it. She asked me "why do you not write books with all of your D&D materials and adventures?" At first I was unsure but she nagged... oops... encouraged me to do so. Now seven books later and I am writing book 8 with Laura still proofreading my chapters as I go.

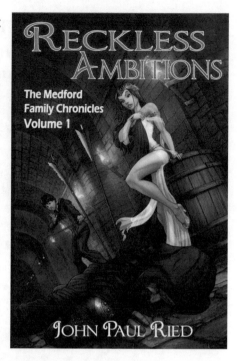

How easy was the shift from dungeonmaster to novelist and what sparked you to do that?

Surprisingly easy. I had and still do have ample amounts of material and being a writer is like being a deity who controls everything and builds a fantasy world. Just like a dungeon master or gamemaster.

How important are your ongoing campaigns to your stories or are they just a backdrop?

Vital. Many of my characters in my books are characters from my adventures with players. I change enough and alter items to suit. More then a backdrop, my campaigns and my extensive Palamar homebrew multiverse is my setting.

As a DM, how do you resist more worldbuilding to focus on personal human stories?

I have hundreds of settings in different climates and cultures so my book writing only develops my D&D homebrew world. I go for "realistic fantasy", and give my characters the spotlight as they adventure, stumble, react and love as they move forwards.

Who's your favorite character, not including your avatar, Oliver Wendell Enalan, and why?

In my books, I am told that my lady characters 'steal the show', and manipulate their men into all sorts of disasters. My favorite lady character is the Anti-Paladin Lydia Jalen Sukurova from my book entitled *Unexpected Entanglements*. She is the quintessential wicked, sexy, vicious warrior woman who will rip anyone to pieces those who stand in her way getting what she wants. My favorite male character is the elderly imperial palace gardener Andrew Lovel Numil who is 'just a simple gardener and healer', and in charge of the Imperial Palamaran Spy System. The IPSS. No one wishes to stand under them and get... um... wet.

How far ahead are you thinking for this series? RPGs can last for a very long time indeed.

One thing I am blessed with is that I never have writer's block. I have endless materials, world building, character development, moral dilemmas, chaos and attempts at order to write about. I will write books until I drop dead which I hope is a very long time off. I already have thousands of years of history and can move forward at will. My first book *Reckless Ambitions* has even an appendix like Tolkien's *Lord of the Rings* books.

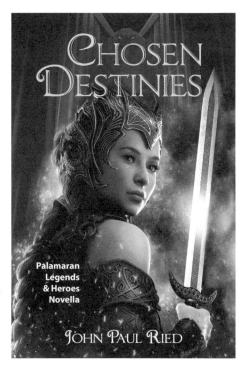

What are your favorite books of the last five years, not including your own?

Ms. Patti Hultstrand, my publisher, dear friend and fellow author, has written numerous books and I try to emulate her writing style along with other authors like James Clavell (*Shogun*) and Isaac Asimov (*Foundation* saga). Ms. Hulstrand's *Romantic Time Travel Saga*, starting with *Battle for Time*, is definitely one favorite that stands out.

And finally, name one other Arizona author that people should absolutely check out.

I just did. Ms. Patti Hulstrand is a wonderful author and I give all her books my highest recommendation for anyone to enjoy. Her *Time Travel Saga* and her *Lizzy/Dark Triangle* books are splendid for anyone who enjoys our fantasy fiction genre.

facebook.com/profile.php?id=100082526574697
x.com/johnpaulried

BIBLIOGRAPHIES

Dani Hoots

A Falling Starr (2014)

The Legend of Akikumo (2020)

A World of Vampires:

A World of Vampires Volume 1 (2014)

A World of Vampires Volume 2 (2015)

Sanshlian Series:

The Quest (2015)

The Journey (2020)

The Return (2020)

Daughter of Hades:

Endangered (2016)

Engaged (2020)

Entangled (2020)

Enchanted (2020)

Wonderland Chronicles:

Trapped in Wonderland (2017)

Captured in Wonderland (2020)

Betrayed in Wonderland (2021)

Transformed in Wonderland (2021)

Last of the Gargoyles:

The Chained (2020)

The Turned (2021)

The Redeemed (2021)

City of Kaus:

Revenge (2021)

Retribution (2022)

Rescue (2022)

Reunion (2022)

Queen of the Underworld:

Tartarus (2021)

Elysium (2021)

Honor Trilogy (as Lyra Thorsson):

The Death of Honor (2021)

The Truth of Honor (2021)

The Price of Honor (2022)

S. C. Mendes

The Little Season (2024)

The City Saga:

The City (2017)

The Order of Eternal Sleep (2022)

with Nikki Noir:

The Lockdown (2020)

Petite Mort (2022)

Suck-U-Bus (2023)

Ernest Hogan

Cortez on Jupiter (1990)

High Aztech (1992)

Smoking Mirror Blues (2001)

Guerrilla Mural of a Siren's Song (2023)

Mona Ventress

Lover of Mythic Propotions:

Anointed by Anubis (2022)

Buzzed on Bacchus (2022)

Creating Centaurs (2022)

Diddlin' the Dryad (2024)

John Paul Ried

The Medford Family Chronicles:

Reckless Ambitions (2015)

Capricious Deities (2016)

Pivotal Ruckus (2017)

Academic Mayhem (2019)

Palamaran Legends and Heroes:

Unexpected Entanglements (2021)

Twisted Timeline (2022)

Palamaran Novellas and Short Stories:

Chosen Destinies (2023)

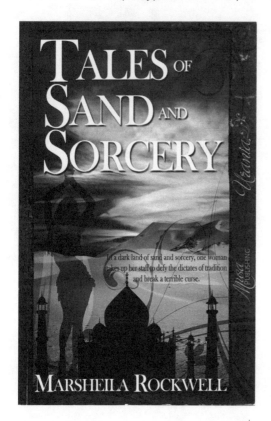

MARSHEILA ROCKWELL

TALES OF SAND AND SORCERY

PUBLISHER:
MUSA
PUBLICATION DATE:
MARCH 2013

I took far too long to get round to reading Marsheila Rockwell's *Legacy of Wolves*, likely because of personal snobbery about modern shared universe stories. However, get round to it I did and I found myself mightily impressed. It and Al Ewing's *Gods of Manhattan* currently reside at the back of my brain where they chip away at my idiocy and gradually persuade me that there are such creatures worth the effort.

So I didn't hesitate when I saw this one. This slim but substantial volume contains seven short stories which fall firmly into old school sword-and-sorcery, though I was surprised to discover that Rockwell's chief inspiration was far from literary. Instead she was inspired by a martial dance, which tradition decrees is only allowed to be performed by men.

Needless to say, she promptly redresses that gender imbalance by conjuring up a female character to dance that dance. And, when she did, she also found that sword and sorcery was a natural fit.

This lead is no musclebound barbarian with sinews of iron; she's a sultan's daughter who disobeyed her father and so was cursed for her trouble. While legend suggests that she was literally turned into a stone fountain, in truth she was cast out and stripped of her ability to feel either pain or pleasure, along with a few syllables from her name, which is much more important than it might seem.

In this world, the length of a name signifies its owner's status, so our warrior princess lost much with her fall from Shaalaraharrah, the

Sultan's Daughter, to the much shorter *Shaala, Made of Stone*.

Now she wanders the desert searching for a way to lift her curse and, naturally, running into a succession of adventures in the process. Each of these works well as a standalone story but also serves as a jigsaw piece. Put together, they show a number of bigger pictures, not all of Shaala herself but never diverting far from her. Another thread follows Kij, a fascinating character in her own right who suffers her own fall in stature and searches for her own release. Naturally the two gravitate together and become travelling companions.

The world they enliven is a character in itself with Rockwell's world-building talents put to frequent use. We discover a host of characters, cities and cultures, each unique and interesting but all the more so because of how they interlock with each other. As we follow the separate but entwined story arcs of Shaala and Kij, key locations flit in and out of our focus and we find ourselves watching them grow in our minds as well. For instance, the city of Samarkesh is introduced in the tangential tale, *The Jade and Honey Harlot*, but our leads find themselves paying it a visit in *Shaala and the Harlot Queen of Sumarkesh*.

Rockwell is a writer of many strengths but three stand supreme. She creates gloriously three-dimensional characters, who come alive for us quickly but grow continually. She's able to bring her stories to life too, creating new ones but somehow making them seem as old as the hills, part of the collective culture of the new worlds she creates. Finally, but perhaps most notably, her use of language is without parallel in the writing community; her prose is enough to tell us that she's a poet at heart and I've long thought that poets often write the

best prose simply because they focus so much on choice and placement of words.

Put together, a growing set of linked stories is the perfect format for each of those talents to shine brightest. I enjoyed *Legacy of Wolves* but much more for her writing than for the world in which it was set; I felt no draw at all towards the rest of that shared world. Here I immediately wanted more; turning the last page carried the acute pain of loss because there was no further adventure to visit.

Or at least not yet. There's plenty of growth room for Rockwell to continue to visit the world of Shaala and Kij and I hope she does so often, turning out more short stories in and amongst the grander projects she's finding herself part of. Adding a note much later than the review, I believe the plan is to adapt this into a fixup novel and work has been done, but it isn't priority because other projects pay money and this one hasn't found a home yet. I hope it does soon.

Given the sheer breadth of approaches that she takes here, from action-based adventure in the time honoured pulp style to accidental forays into folklore, from deep dives into fascinating fictional or fictionalised cultural traditions to fireside stories that she appears to have narrated onto the page, it would seem to be a likelihood that Shaala and/or Kij will appear in anthologies to come because they're flexible enough to fit in a fistful of places. I look forward to visiting all of them.

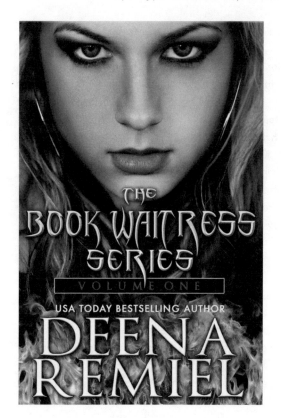

DEENA REMIEL

THE BOOK WAITRESS VOLUME ONE

THE BOOK WAITRESS #1

PUBLISHER:
FIREWALKER PRESS

PUBLICATION DATE:
APRIL 2013

I'm not used to either reading or reviewing paranormal romance, the closest to which I've got in the past is likely Laurell K. Hamilton's lycanthropic porn novels midway through her *Anita Blake* series. I liked Deena Remiel's pitch for this set of three novellas at a local author event though and finally found an appropriate way to read it, by candlelight during a twelve-hour power outage.

What surprised me, not being familiar with the genre, was how familiar it felt, rather like one of Graham Masterton's horror novels with the inevitable hero moving to a new town where he finds both demonic horror and a pretty girl in a cool job. His heroines tended to run seaside antiques stores, but Camille Dutton is a librarian. Not worthy, not worthy.

She's at once the leading lady and the damsel in distress, while Derek, her new boyfriend, fits closer to the Masterton hero mold.

He's an investigative journalist, on Shelter Island because he believes that its satanic cult, supposedly defunct for three decades, has continued in secret to kidnap and murder a young boy every six years in a ritual sacrifice to the Lord of Darkness. What's more, it's been six years since the last and there's a new boy missing. Naturally Derek is right, but he's still surprised to discover that the librarian he meets while doing research on his first day is the secondary sacrifice, having already been marked by Satan as a six-year-old.

Of course, the horror is toned down and the romance toned up from the formula I'm used to, but that doesn't quite capture it. There's plenty of horror here, especially given that Camille gets carved up by a plastic surgeon until her body is covered in pentagrams and inverted crosses and the like. However, the way it's treated is more like a network TV show than something you might see on HBO. Similarly, the romance is certainly toned up but the sex is toned down, this being low on the Scoville scale of smuttiness that I believe paranormal romances tend to be measured by. There's nothing sizzling off the page here, and the interplay between the lead characters unfolds continually in slow motion with hair blowing in the wind and a saxophone underpinning it all. At least that's how I read it.

Maybe the lack of sex is because of all those pentagrams and inverted crosses. They don't just cause pain because, well, they'd be frickin' painful. They also mark the entry into our world of another demon and Camille feels that transition thirteen times a day. Put together, that's believably enough to stop anyone jumping in the sack with her hot boyfriend.

It moves along well enough and kept me interested throughout. The biggest flaw to me is probably the biggest boon to the target audience, so it's an easy task to forgive that, namely that Camille and Derek are of course young and incredibly hot, the social awkwardness they share hindering their immediate attraction to each other but with the likelihood that they'll eventually hook up being a near certainty. Their social awkwardness does seem to come and go, but it's there during the many moments they might hook up, thus taking a lot longer than it should in the holy name of romantic tension.

What doesn't stand up as well is just how young they are. Camille is 24 years old, an important age because it's divisible by six, and Derek seems to be around the same. I'd have bought into the story a lot more if they'd been a decade or so older. Camille at 36 would have been even more attractive to Satan, as it's six times six, and I might have been able to buy into her bank balance. Similarly, Derek would have seemed more believable in his thirties, given his job experience and connections to people who can help when Camille decides to fight back and he decides to be her sidekick.

The other obvious flaw is one that may be inherent in the fact that this book, which runs just shy of three hundred pages, is really three books in one, hence the unwieldy title. *The Book Waitress Series Volume One* is hardly enticing, but *The Book Waitress*, *Devil du Jour* and *Demon a la Mode* are much more like it. Each of them merely takes the form of a novella rather than a novel, so there's not too

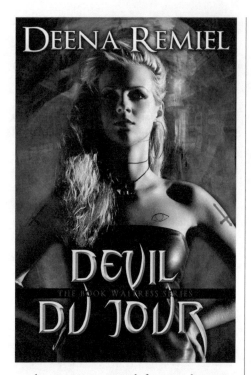

things are going to go down and the third adds a new wildcard of a character to the mix just to keep things interesting by introducing romantic conflict.

It feels like the set-up is finally complete as of the end of the third novella, so book four ought to be the first run-of-the mill episode, leading us into a mix of good or bad books, depending on the week. The whole thing feels so much like a TV show that I'm already picturing the guest stars and missing a book or two because of a baseball game or a political primary. It's no surprise to pull up Remiel's website and discover that she aims *The Book Waitress* at being a thirteen novella series in the spirit of her favorite shows, *Buffy the Vampire Slayer*, *Angel* and *Charmed*.

much opportunity in each for Remiel to write in complexity.

Therefore we're never surprised at who turns out to be what, because we're effectively introduced only to the characters that matter. Nobody is here without a reason and, beyond Cynthia and Derek, there's only one reason to be in the story, for at least the first novella. Even in the second and third, the new characters are either obviously on the side of the protagonists or worshippers of Satan and it's pretty obvious from moment one which each of them will be. There's simply no room for any other characters to find a foothold.

What Remiel does well is build the story. While the first part is self-contained, it plays like the pilot to a TV series, introducing all the key characters and the back story; then setting us up for the many episodes to come. The second part builds the framework for how

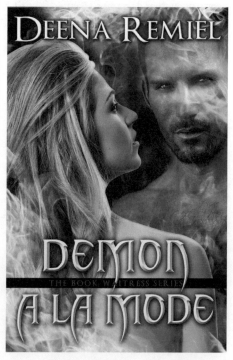

JOANNA SENGER

BETRAYAL, BETROTHAL, AND BLOOD

HERMIONE DAGGERT #1

PUBLISHER:
NIGHT TO DAWN

PUBLICATION DATE:
JUNE 2014

I enjoyed JoAnna Senger's debut novel (which she's been waiting to write for far too long) a great deal, even if I felt like I shouldn't. It has a horrible, if colorful, cover and it feels like she broke a whole lot of rules in writing it. My OCD and my subconscious kept triggering as if something was wrong, making it an odd read, but it's a good one nonetheless.

Perhaps I should attempt to define what it is, because it kept me on the hop for a while my first time through, trying to figure it out.

Senger herself suggests it's a "dark murder mystery" and I suppose that's true. However, of those three words, "murder" is the only one that's really beyond doubt as the book does revolve around a set of murders committed at Milady's Manor, a flamboyant hotel in the small Californian town of San Tobino. Milady's is a colourful place, each room decorated to a different theme, and someone is bumping off the clientèle in accordance with those themes.

As the neatly alliterative title hints, there is a darkness to it, but it's neither told as a horror story nor a thriller, though Senger wouldn't have found it difficult at all to delve deeper into that darkness. It is a mystery in the sense that the majority of the key characters are tasked with solving the murders at Milady's. However, it's not a mystery to us for long because Senger quickly explains to us whodunit and doesn't wait too long before leaving us in no doubt as to why.

This led me to wonder if it was going to be a police procedural, with Detectives Karl Kelly and Vito Kostowski struggling to find any-thing that might link the growing number of victims together. They aren't bad cops but this is small town California where murders don't tend to happen, so they're immediately out of their depth and they know it; but, they're still responsible for bringing in the perpetrator. However, we never focus enough on the cops to regard them as the driving force of the story, or at least the only driving force of the story, and the coroner and others who would fit into that procedural framework are kept at a minimum.

At one point it hints at becoming a legal drama, but it never does much more than that, even within the courtroom. There's so much more going on at this point in the story that keeps our attention even as the alleged killer is suffering through his trial.

What it really boils down to is a character study. We're here to observe, even as most of the characters we observe are busy observing themselves. We don't watch Kelly and Kostow-ski run through a literary take on *CSI*, we watch them flounder around trying to figure out what they're missing. Their eyes are well and truly open but they don't see what they need to. We're not puzzling with them because we know what they're not seeing, but we watch through their eyes anyway to find a realization as to why they're stuck.

There are a couple of other detectives in the mix too. One is a private investigator called Emma Denning, an odd but sharp bird whose years inside don't match those outside. She's in her mid-thirties but she dresses out of the Victorian era, without any reasons given as to why. It's just who she is, which is appreciated, and we watch closely to learn more about her during those moments when the cops call her

in for assistance.

The other doesn't become a professional until Senger's second novel, but she practices her observational skills throughout, even solving an unrelated minor crime partway through. She's Hermione Daggert, a waitress at Milady's, whose diary entries are peppered through the book, especially those which talk about the two regulars who crop up again and again in each of the threads of this story. She calls one of them Lord Byron and the other His Grayness; both are keen observers too. This side of the story is as close as this gets to a cosy, though Hermione is neither the only major character nor the dominant one.

Given that this is all about observation, we can't fail to do that and see a lot more than just the story in the process.

The worst thing about the book is easily its presentation. Beyond the poor cover art, the proofing is substandard, with a wildly incon-sistent use of smart quotes; the name of one of the lead characters is even missing a letter in the back cover blurb. On a more subjective level, the headers are too prominent and the indents too deep. The headers are centered but the footers pushed to the outer margins. My British schooling even rails at the Oxford comma in the book's title.

Another thing that many may see as a negative, but I don't, is the consistently chan-ging point of view. We don't look at this story from any one perspective. Karl and Vito's investigation is one thread, told entirely from Karl's perspective in the third person. We're also given two other perspectives in the third person, from a husband and wife whose lives are moving further apart. Hermione's diaries, however, are told in the first person. This odd mixture of perspectives isn't likely to be what most readers are going to expect and they may well find it awkward. The odd concept of justice that Senger plays with may not meet all tastes either. However, I particularly appreciated all of this for being notable breaths of fresh air in a formula-ridden genre.

The strongest part is undoubtedly Senger's insight. Any character study lives or dies on its writer's insight and I'm happy to underline just how well she does. It's a good job because, in truth, we're observing her observing her characters observing other characters and

that sort of nesting has to be done right or it'll all fall apart horribly. It works wonderfully.

I'd highly recommend that, if you're a mystery buff who wants something a little different from the formulaic norm, you look past the gaudy cover of this book and see if it shakes up your expectations of what you'll read in the future by showing you how the rules can be broken without sacrificing value. I've just enjoyed it as much on a return visit to prepare me for Senger's second book, *Reservation Ravaged*.

JOANNA SENGER

RESERVATION RAVAGED

HERMIONE DAGGERT #2

PUBLISHER:
NIGHT TO DAWN
PUBLICATION DATE:
JUNE 2014

I enjoyed JoAnna Senger's first "dark murder mystery" a great deal, not only because it didn't follow the standard rules but certainly in large part because of that. I enjoyed her second too, for many of the same reasons, but

it plays its cards a little more conventionally than the first and so I found that I didn't enjoy it quite as much.

Senger doesn't write traditional mysteries. Her debut novel, *Betrayal, Betrothal, and Blood*, was above all a character study, in which we observe the writer observing her characters observing other characters. That's an intriguing concept, if not a traditional one. There is a mystery at the heart of its story, a set of obscure murders that are investigated by some of the characters and which are solved in the end, if not in a traditional way.

Now she's back with book two, *Reservation Ravaged*, which isn't particularly traditional either, not even in being a sequel. However, it is a little more traditional than its predecessor, as we do at least spend the majority of the book following a single detective as she investigates a single crime, yet another set of murders. Where things depart from the norm are in the way she does this, how the mysteries in the book are solved and, once again, in the overarching feel of what Senger's trying to do with her writing.

That detective is Hermione Daggert, a waitress in the first book who solves an incidental crime and ends up involved in the main one, outstripping the cops with her observational skills. By the time this second book begins, she's completed three years of training to become the partner of Emma Denning, the only private investigator we know in the small Californian town of San Tobino and surely the most colorful. The cops she helped out last time around, Detectives Karl Kelly and Vito Kostowski, return too, as does the hotel of Milady's, where the murders of that book happened and where Hermione used to work. All of these are very much subservient characters this time out though.

The company of Denning and Daggert is initially hired to look into the strange case of land on an Indian reservation which has suddenly fallen into uncharacteristic decline,

but this is only the framing story and it's apparently wrapped up quickly enough. The real mystery arrives after Hermione solves the case, the Kanache tribe sell their blighted land and the buyer, Dr. Frederick Unlickner, builds the Institute for Holistic Health on it. A set of grisly accidents promptly befall the institute, pretty young things falling into ravines, often with lockpicks stuck into them, and it just may well be that none of them are really accidents, so Hermione is sent undercover to figure out what's really going on.

The most successful aspects of the book are the ones that are reminiscent from its predecessor. Senger's prose is smooth but insightful, her sentences crafted with carefully chosen vocabulary and a very capable turn of phrase; it wouldn't surprise me if she also writes poetry. She crafts her dialogue in a much more literary style than contemporary American writers tend to use, but she successfully keeps it realistic. I'm all for the approach.

Her characters are written deeply, though not in the usual way. Senger doesn't introduce them with standard descriptions like, "she was 5'4" with mousy brown hair and a tattoo of a flower on her left wrist." In fact, she mostly eschews physical attributes entirely, drawing her characters instead from deeper observations, so that we understand precisely who they are without having much clue what they look like.

The presentation is a little better than last time, although the cover design is still poor. A larger font size minimizes the other issues my OCD had with the design of the first book, even if most are still apparent. The text looks good and is thankfully well-proofed this time around. The use of smart quotes is consistent here at least, hallelujah!

The negative side is going to be difficult to explain without resorting to spoilers because it's mostly apparent through hindsight once the book is done, but I'll give it a go. Many might see it revolving around Senger's refusal to yet again play this out as a straight mystery, focusing far more on developing her protagonist than her mystery. The framing story, with its supernatural flavour, renders that approach even less tangible, meaning that this is just as far from a recognizable mystery as her first book.

Hermione doesn't merely avoid summoning everyone together at the end of the book to reveal the killer, as if this could ever be mistaken for an Agatha Christie novel. She doesn't follow clues or draw up lists of suspects either and even as an undercover PI she avoids sticking her nose in and stirring things up. She's perhaps the most passive PI I've ever read and that's fine, except that Senger's skills of observation are focused more on her than on anyone else.

For my part, the negative side is in how we assign value to what we read. The highly unorthodox way in which the killer is "caught" in *Betrayal, Betrothal, and Blood* sets the scene for this one, in which our mystery transforms into a thriller and then wraps itself up with short shrift. We don't wonder about what we've read but we do wonder about why we read it. If the ending could have happened at any point in time with exactly the same result, why did we read what we read up to that point?

Well, that would be a valid concern if this were a mystery first and foremost, as indeed it's marketed and tends to be described. Senger calls her novels "dark murder mys-teries", but while they certainly include those elements, they're not the driving ones. As with her first book, this is above all a character study, something that really should be shelved in general fiction rather than mystery or crime, for all that the story revolves around a set of murders. We're never here to solve anything; we're here to observe Hermione Daggert as she goes about her business observing other people and the value in the book is in how her character develops.

Like *Betrayal, Betrothal, and Blood*, this flows well and keeps our interest throughout, but isn't phrased in the sort of way that mystery fans are likely to appreciate. At points, this could be described as a thriller, a horror story or a drama, but it's never eager to really be a mystery. Its value is in Senger's writing, relentlessly unorthodox approach and, above all, her ability to observe. Armchair detectives need not apply.

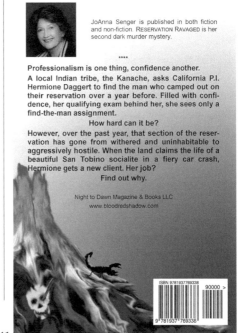

JoAnna Senger is published in both fiction and non-fiction. RESERVATION RAVAGED is her second dark murder mystery.

****

Professionalism is one thing, confidence another.
A local Indian tribe, the Kanache, asks California P.I. Hermione Daggert to find the man who camped out on their reservation over a year before. Filled with confidence, her qualifying exam behind her, she sees only a find-the-man assignment.
How hard can it be?
However, over the past year, that section of the reservation has gone from withered and uninhabitable to aggressively hostile. When the land claims the life of a beautiful San Tobino socialite in a fiery car crash, Hermione gets a new client. Her job?
Find out why.

Night to Dawn Magazine & Books LLC
www.bloodredshadow.com

ISBN 9781937769338

9 781937 769338

90000 >

BETH CATO

THE CLOCKWORK DAGGER

OCTAVIA LEANDER #1

PUBLISHER:
HARPERCOLLINS

PUBLICATION DATE:
SEPTEMBER 2014

After thoroughly enjoying Viola Carr's *The Diabolical Miss Hyde*, I decided that I should follow with Beth Cato's *The Clockwork Dagger*, because the two books seemed to have much in common.

Both are new novels from Harper Voyager, written by female authors who had not been published before, at least not under these names. Both are multi-genre period adventures, Victorian effectively if not strictly, with strong female leads. Both even feature cover illustrations that scream romance, though it isn't main drive of either book. And, of course, both are of interest to the steampunk scene.

What I found was that those similarities were very high level and this book turned out to remind far more of *Dreadnought*, the second book in Cherie Priest's noted *Clockwork Century* series, because it follows the same template throughout, if in a more episodic, cliffhanger sort of way.

Both *Dreadnought* and *The Clockwork Dagger* are set during a time of war, though Priest chose to fictionalise real history by setting her book during the American Civil War while Cato created an entirely fictional war in an entirely fictional world, with the country of Caskentia years into a long and protracted conflict with the Dallows, which is also known in derogatory fashion as the Waste, which apparently describes the place well.

Both revolve around a leading lady who works in the medical field and is stubbornly but professionally unwilling to discriminate between sides. Priest placed her nurse, Mercy Lynch, under the Confederate flag while her husband had died for the Union. Cato's medician, Octavia Leander, finds safety and danger from both sides, not least because the man she finds that she can trust the most, Alonzo Garret, the Clockwork Dagger of the title, a Caskentian secret agent masquerading as an airship steward, is the son of the very Dallows general who caused the death of her entire family and her entire town.

Both characters find their stories explored during long and dangerous cross-country treks. Lynch follows the summons of her dying father from Virginia to Washington state, initially by airship and boat but mostly on the train of the title. Leander has been tasked with saving the stricken people of Delford, a long way from the city of Vorana where she climbs on board the airship on which she'll remain for most of her journey south. Incidentally, this airship is even named *Argus* to highlight how epic this journey will be, as we can be sure that it's not going to be a relaxing ride.

Both also tell grounded, dramatic stories but bring in a single fantastic element to spice things up. Priest's are the zombies created through contact with the gas seeping out of the Seattle ground. Cato's is the use of magic, Leander's powers sourced from the Lady and the Tree, which may or may not equate to the same thing in her pagan religion which intriguingly adds some Eastern elements to its Celtic roots. There's also Leaf, the baby gremlin that she rescues from a bludgeoning party and with whom she somehow bonds. He's a wild element who gets little to do here but may well get plenty in future episodes.

They're far from the same book, of course. Cato's prose aims far more for adventure than literature; she writes well but isn't trying to escape her genre, while Priest's eloquence is a sure sign that she's trying to write the great American novel, merely with zombies. Cato's lead is much younger, so there's also romance that's mostly missing from *Dreadnought*.

What's more, she adds a further complication which manifests in the form of Leander's roommate on board the Argus, a complication which will surely become far more prominent in future books. Priest's novel was primarily a character study of her heroine, making little attempt to connect her adventures with the wider world she had created in *Boneshaker*. Cato's builds Leander and her world together with further books very much in mind. *The Clockwork Dagger* works well as a standalone novel, but is clearly intended just as deliberately as the first book in a series.

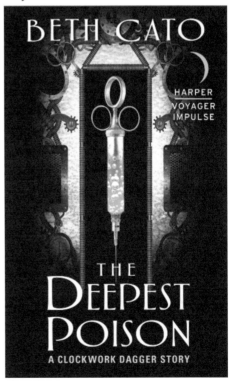

43

I enjoyed *The Clockwork Dagger* a great deal and am looking forward to *The Clockwork Crown*, due in June (*The Deepest Poison*, a short story, will predate it in April). There's a lot of potential for the world to grow enough that this book might seem like a small thing indeed once it's done. For now, it's substantial and consistent, with a host of worthy characters.

Chief among them, of course, is the medician, a multi-faceted heroine who stands out among her peers not because of her looks but because of her character. She's endearingly unaware of how special she truly is and has difficulty coming to terms with the revealed truth that so many people are indeed after her, whether to capture her, kill her or keep her safe. In other hands this can often seem forced but Cato has no trouble keeping her lead believable indeed. The biggest stretch is

surely her use of magic because it's entirely wrapped up in her religion and we often forget that this is a fantasy as much as it is a dramatic adventure because nobody else is doing anything similar.

As strong as she is, she would also be clearly dead many times over from the flurry of attacks aimed her way if it wasn't for Alonzo Garret. While he is often phrased like a prince coming to her rescue, she's thankfully never a damsel in distress; she's too busy being the prince coming to the rescue of others because those attacks are aimed widely enough to not include her alone in their scope.

Mrs Viola Stout is the third of these key characters, Leander's roommate on board the *Argus*. It's clear from the outset that she isn't only the rich widow who enjoys travelling, but the reveal is a capable one which sets the tone for many similarly capable reveals later in the book. This is a world at war and, as publicity might say, it's dripping with intrigue. The game is afoot, nobody is who they seem and only the Shadow knows. Cato is far from the first writer to venture into this sort of cliffhanger territory but she does it well enough and adds texture through her characters and the cities they journey through.

I may be biased towards Beth because she brings cookies to her book signings and they are, as they say, to die for, but this is a worthy read for anyone who wants a little romance in their adventure, a lot of adventure in their romance and a dash of fantasy to spruce it all up. *The Clockwork Dagger* gets dark on occasion (heck, it begins with a puppy being run over) but it refuses to stay there. It's a lighter and more conventional read than *The Diabolical Miss Hyde* but it should please a lot of the same readers.

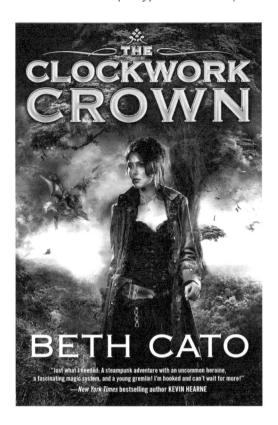

BETH CATO

THE CLOCKWORK CROWN

OCTAVIA LEANDER #2

PUBLISHER:
HARPERCOLLINS

PUBLICATION DATE:
JUNE 2015

I enjoyed *The Clockwork Dagger*, Beth Cato's first adventure for medician Octavia Leander, a great deal, but felt that it drew a little too much on its most obvious influence and ended a little abruptly. This second half to Octavia's story, which is firmly ended after two books, takes a few chapters to find its feet but then really finds them, blistering through to a very strong conclusion with panache.

I devoured the first book relatively quickly, wanting to know how it would progress, but I didn't find it difficult to put it down so I could sleep. Once I got my teeth into *The Clockwork Crown*, I was hooked and read the second half in a single sitting, through to OMG o'clock in the morning.

With many secrets revealed by the end of the first book, everyone involved is acutely aware of where they stand when the second gets moving and we're well framed for the story to come.

Octavia is absolutely on the run, both from agents of the Caskentian crown and their Waster foes in the Dallows, but Alonzo Garret is just as firmly on the run with her, no longer a Clockwork Dagger because of his choice to put her safety before his duties as a spy and killer. With the powers of two nations arrayed against them, they head south to a third, his home country, hoping to find some downtime to regroup and do much needed research on the Lady, her Tree and what the bigger story around them truly is. However, adventure and danger are never far away and our heroes are

HARPER
VOYAGER
IMPULSE

Collected together for the first time, three works of short fiction, including the Nebula Award-nominated novella *Wings of Sorrow and Bone*

inevitably back off and running again, but rarely in the ways we might expect.

Everything about *The Clockwork Crown* feels stronger and more assured than in the prior book, because Cato's writing is stronger and far more assured. While the first novel was capably constructed, it felt constructed with the progression of the leads through a set of cliffhangers paramount and other supporting characters only there to allow that to happen. Here, the story is far more fluid, going wherever it must rather than merely to the next point of peril.

While I enjoyed the characters in *The Clockwork Dagger*, the leads found direction here and the supporting characters their own real places in the bigger story too.

Octavia has grown massively as a character between the first and second books, though she's struggling with the similar growth of her abilities as a magical healer. Given that her talents, which memorably allow her to hear the pain of those around her in musical form, were trouble for her in built up areas even at the start of her story, but their enhancement becomes a downright danger as they arrive in Tamarania. She learns a lot in the south, about who she is and what role she is to play in the world. We learn with her and are thankful.

Alonzo Garret ran dangerously close to a romantic dream in the first book, but he grows here too and their connection grows as well while successfully avoiding overt sentimentality. It's telling that, while he does get a few occasions to strut his stuff as a tough cookie, not least in an outrageous robotic tournament to the death, he clearly plays second fiddle to Octavia, even when protecting her. While she was never just a damsel in distress, that's a welcome reversal of their roles.

Other characters gain welcome depth too, whether expanded from their roles in the first book or introduced in this one. They each have a natural place in this story, even the ones that I didn't see coming. Tatiana Garret, the precocious ten year old sister of Alonzo, is a scene-stealing star, but she's only one of a wide variety of new faces, including Tamaranian kingpin, Balthazar Cody; Viola Stout's obnoxious son, Devin; and others whom I can't mention without venturing firmly into spoiler territory.

In fact I can't mention quite a lot, because you deserve to discover these characters and progressions yourself. One key progression is telegraphed a little early, meaning that it's nowhere near as surprising to us as it is to the characters when it becomes too obvious for

46

them to ignore, but there are others sprung magnificently on us and the characters both. I'd imagined certain scenes in this book even while finishing up the first one, but I was happily surprised when they turned out to be nothing like I expected.

In fact, my biggest mistake was to imagine this as a series. *The Clockwork Dagger* often felt like a long introduction to a set of characters who only found their feet during the finalé. With a whole wide world ready to be unveiled, I expected a host of future books to flesh out the map and give the characters room enough to breathe and grow. *The Clockwork Crown* only hints at the wider map but still wraps up Octavia's story with comfort and style as a firm duology.

It would be possible for Cato to write further books in this world, but they would be new stories. Just as the first book was a beginning, this is very much an ending and it plays strong enough to deserve not to become just a chapter in the middle.

The good news is that, while this may be the end to Octavia's story, it's surely not the end to Cato's writing. I can envision *The Clockwork Dagger* being remembered as her first book, an achievement to be proud of but mostly for being the first with her name on the front. *The Clockwork Crown* will have a lot more resonance, marking the point where she become comfortable with her writing and able to become the conduit for a story inside her to flow onto the page.

Here's to this story not being the last, because I'm eager to see what Beth Cato will do next. It's wonderful to watch an author find her voice, but it's even better to read what that voice has to say.

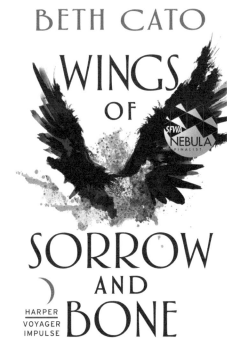

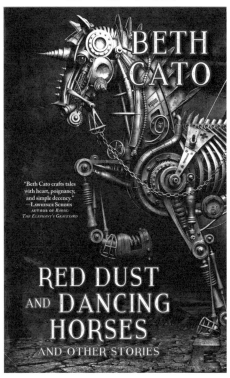

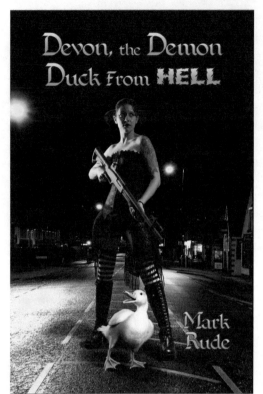

MARK RUDE

DEVON, THE DEMON DUCK FROM HELL

PUBLISHER:
DUCK CASTLE PRESS

PUBLICATION DATE:
APRIL 2013

This self-published novel by Mark Rude is a huge amount of fun and I'd recommend it highly to anyone with a sense of humour, not only those who will understand the local jibes. I'm completely sold on the revelations about Scottsdale that Mr. Rude unfurls midway through the book and I bet they won't be a surprise to anyone else living here in the Valley of the Sun.

It didn't take that to sell me on the book though. I was sold merely by reading the back cover blurb, with its quotes from reviewers at the *Afterlife Times*. Just so you don't miss out on the experience, here they are:

"Villainous!" - William Shakespeare
"Blasphemous!" - Pope John Paul II
"Senseless!" - Jane Austen
"Duck!" - John F. Kennedy

Oh yeah, if you're not bent over double and creased up with laughter after that little gem, this may not be the book for you. If you are, as I've found most people I ask to read the back cover aloud tend to be, it certainly is.

We begin in northern Arizona, in the town of Bueller (anyone, anyone?) which doesn't exist outside of the pages of this book. That's a good thing because Bueller is the sort of place where university students like to conduct rituals to raise demons in the tunnels under the school, rituals that involve live animal sacrifices. What brings them down is that the particular ritual they're using has been tampered with, so the demons they raise inhabit clones of the sacrifices, without the cultists having much of a clue what's happened. After all, they don't speak duck.

Devon, as the title suggests, is a demon raised through the sacrifice of a duck and so that's the form which he gets to inhabit on our plane and, well, he's not particularly chuffed about that. As you can imagine, nobody else speaks duck either.

Well, except Annie Puckett.

Annie is a Goth chick, meaning that she's already out of place in Bueller, and she doesn't exactly win friends and influence people at her job in a local video rental store, but she also happens to have a particularly useful tattoo on the back of her neck, as Devon discovers by accident when he sees him waddling along outside her store. By the glorious powers of coincidence, the tattoo turns out to be the sigil of Babel, a.k.a. the Demon of Many Tongues, which her tattoo artist had found in a bunch of clipart on the net.

That means that Annie becomes Devon's way home. Or, as he puts it, "I require your assistance to exact my revenge and return to Hell." He's pushy like that. It also means, along with some more revelations that I won't spoil, that there's a conspiracy going on that involves very important people, the world wide web and those pesky end user license agreements that none of us ever bother to read. Well, if Devon is a trustworthy duck, we'd better start reading them right now but it's already too late for our mortal souls. Hell, people believe in a lot wackier books than this one, so who's to say that Rude doesn't have it right. It makes logical sense to me.

There's a lot to enjoy here, but most of it revolves around the dark and surreal humour. After all, it starts out with a demon-possessed duck and gets more progressively fantastic from there, so grounding in reality is not high on Mark Rude's priority list. Top is having fun with pop culture references, to be followed in no particular order by a neat sense of irony, ever increasing surreality and the ability to poke fun at Arizona stereotypes by raising cynical truths. Puns are certainly up there too and the willingness to name characters just to generate quality chapter names out of them. On each of those fronts, Rude rocks royally.

There is a downside, but it's hardly important. The left hand pages have mangled margins, meaning that the text is too near the spine, but it's readable and probably annoys me more than most because of my proofreader's OCD. Each chapter is heralded by an amateur charcoal drawing and I didn't like them from moment one, though they did grow on me before I ran out of pages.

More notably, there are more than a few plot conveniences to put up with, but I've read many books with more and in a book called *Devon, the Demon Duck from Hell*, they really don't stop us whizzing along eagerly from page 1 to page 304. The bigger problem is that there isn't a page 305, because this is so much fun that I didn't want it to end.

Fortunately, Mark Rude has published other novels, namely a young adult fantasy series called *The Cindra Corrina Chronicles*. It began before this book with *The Gold Cat's Daughter* and *The Gallant Riders*,' then continued after it. I merely wish that I had a time machine handy so I could travel forward to 2050, pick up all forty of his novels and fly back to devour the lot of them in one blissfully deranged month. Hilariously, that could be the book he's writing right now. What could go wrong?

KHURT KHAVE

CHAINSAW ALICE IN WONDERLAND

PUBLISHER:
CREATESPACE
PUBLICATION DATE:
APRIL 2014

It's surprisingly rare nowadays to see such an honest creature as this in book form, given that it wears its raw intentions in its title and simple but effective cover. Yes, this is the time-honoured story of *Alice in Wonderland*, retold in the style of a punk zine with all the requisite irreverence, right from the "Legal Bullshit" page that precedes the contents.

I know author Khurt Khave well, having co-founded the Arizona Penny Dreadfuls with him and a couple of lovely ladies, and this combines much of what I expected from him in a book titled *Chainsaw Alice in Wonderland*: not just sex and violence in copious quantities, but also steampunk, tea duelling, Nicola Tesla, tentacle porn and the Cthulhu Mythos. After all, one of the most prominent characters in

the book, Dirty Weasel, is only a mildly fictionalised version of the author's tea duelling persona, a legend in his own teatime, so this was always going to be surreal wish fulfilment shenanigans.

Readers of earlier Khave books such as *Something with Blood in the Title* will recognise the punk zine approach which breaks up the text with a wild variety of images trawled out of the public domain, many of them manipulated with satirical or just subversive intent. Khave's punk poetry, all over that book, also features here, albeit in much reduced quantity, merely dotted around here and there.

What's new is the host of pseudoscientific gobbledegook to attempt a vague explanation of what's going on in a metaphysical sci-fi pulp adventure take on the story and some fun play with language in ways that are both adult in nature but childish in approach. To shift sideways into another Victorian children's classic, Khave writes rather like Peter Pan, the child who refuses to grow up but learns all about the adult world anyway.

Lewis Carroll wrote a satire in the form of a children's story and Khave choose to retain his approach, albeit with less pointed satire and a schoolboy's attitude. Alice is cool, but she'd be a lot cooler with a chainsaw, right? What schoolboy wouldn't agree with that?

Khave throws everything but the kitchen sink into his demented subversion of a childhood classic with the tea party chapter epitomising this approach, with each page adding a new subversion. This version is set within the apocalyptic grounds of an insane asylum where the Mad Hatter uses Wonderland tea to date rape Alice on the table, only to be beaten by the Weasel both at tea duelling and with a baseball bat, which debauchery ends with a fairy queefing glitter over the landscape. This is the sort of thing that kids would adore as long as their parents don't have a clue what they're reading.

Technically, it's rough in the way that self-published books often are. There's no justification and paragraphs are indented too far. It's spellchecked but not proofed, as broken indents and incorrect spellings that happen to also be valid words ably highlight. It's clearly unedited, as the first couple of chapters are notably awkward, but it improves from there as Khave found his narrative flow and unleashed a wild imagination that has to be experienced to be believed.

The biggest success is surely Khave's play with language, which is as honest as the cover in that it's literally play. I could easily imagine some sections being braindumps of literary manipulation, often in dialogue as if the characters on the page are different manifestations of suggestions running through his head. He has a particular penchant for alliteration and portmanteau word creation, but also twists both sound and spelling for effect, appropriately enough given the source. He plunders *Jabberwocky* as much as the dictionary for his vocabulary and takes it as a starting point for extrapolation.

Of course, this play is as delightfully inappropriate as everything else. I was rather taken by the jizzemental, hardly the cleverest portmanteau in the book but surely one of its most abiding images. There are many of these, for whom shock factor is more often than not an important component part. Just as you think you've read all that Khave's schoolboy imagination has to offer, he surprises you with something new.

What's important is that it's all done in fun, as much as it is in the holy name of bad taste. Even while tentacle raping a classic work of children's fiction, he somehow never loses respect for what made it so endearing to generations: its childlike wonder at the world, its playful approach to the English language and its unceasing faith in the power of innocence to change the world into whatever we want it to be.

Nowadays, it could be argued that more people know *Alice* from an overdose of Disney marketing and merchandising its characters than from the actual books themselves, but Khave goes back to the source for those endearing traits that made it great, even while he visits a litany of vile and depraved treatments on its characters.

That a book so deliberately irreverent is so innately respectful is perhaps the most surprising thought to come to mind after finishing this debauched romp. I'm sure the Dodgson estate wouldn't find this remotely respectful and Disney would certainly have conniptions. It could be argued that the latter is more than enough recommendation on its own, but I'll add mine anyway.

If you're looking for family friendly entertainment or you're easily offended, this is certainly not the book for you. However if your dark side has a debauched sense of humour, you're likely to have a blast tagging along with Alice and her chainsaw. I'd love to see a film version of this, but while Tim Burton has tried to monopolise dark reinvention of the classics, this is much more suited to the style of Ralph Bakshi and, really, it wouldn't work in live action. It would need to be animated, probably by the Japanese, which would make the translation all the more surreal.

A sequel is apparently coming soon.

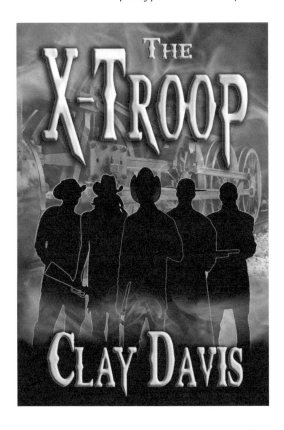

CLAY DAVIS

THE X-TROOP

PUBLISHER:
UNKNOWN
PUBLICATION DATE:
FEBRUARY 2015

Clay Davis is well-known within the Arizona steampunk community, so it's no surprise that this western takes the odd confident step into that genre, albeit not quite as much as I might have expected.

It's perhaps best described as the start to a pulp western series, with a secret organisation of misfits tasked with tackling what ought to be a seemingly unending supply of villains in future books. They are the X-Troop of the title, of course, known officially as the Elite Cavalry Territorial Guard and they're separated from President Ulysses S. Grant by only a single general. Their first opponents are a criminal gang known as the Locusts.

The book succeeds best at framing this pulp team's origin story, to show where the future cycle began and set in motion where it's going. Davis carefully sets up the need for secrecy by explaining away General Custer's death at the Little Bighorn in conspiracy theory terms: he was brave but rash, highlighted not only by the choices in battle that led to his demise but by his raising to Congress corruption that went all the way up to President Grant's brother. If this "threat from within" can't be tackled through appropriate channels, then they must be tackled outside them! After all, that's what we learned from *The Untouchables*, right?

I liked this set-up and I liked where it took us. Davis starts well but gets better as the story builds and the characters begin to find themselves. I only wish they'd had longer to do so and that Davis had spent a little more time in the editing process. Certainly this is a complete novel, with a good first act to introduce the core idea, a decent second as the X-Troop is put together and a strong third as they're thrown into their first real job and, needless to say, come out on top. It's notable also that the action grows consistently from a talky beginning to a wild finale, meaning that the book is hard to put down.

Unfortunately, the drawbacks are often the usual ones for a first-time novelist who's self-publishing his work. The layout is awful, with badly set margins, no justification and awkward page numbering. To play devil's advocate, the proofing is capable and smartquotes and italics are consistent, so it's not all bad on this front. As if to highlight that typographic schizophrenia, the front cover looks great but the back cover is entirely blank. It's hardly surprising to discover that it's basically an e-book thrown at a printer, even if it's a commercial printer that can do binding.

Now if my publisher's eye and rampant OCD for layout can be won over by a good story, that means that *The X-Troop* has something strong going for it. The odd layout makes it difficult for me to gauge the book's true length but it wraps in under a hundred pages and I devoured it in two nights, so it's either a short novel or a novella. I'd like to see it as a regular length novel, though, expanded especially to bolster the characters as there are too many of them to really benefit from this length.

The one who benefits most in this one is the leader of this new band, Colonel Orsen Ritter, who, like Custer, has ended up on the wrong side of bad people in power. He begins the story unfairly behind bars in the military prison at Fort Leavenworth but soon gains release

through the efforts of General Phil Sheridan, who by contrast, begins the story chatting with President Grant on the banks of the Delaware. Ritter is Sheridan's choice to run the X-Troop and he gives him free reign to populate it.

And so Sheridan exits stage left, only a few chapters in, so that Ritter can take over and build his team. While Davis ably uses this point to set up a number of important things to the story, I'd have been happier if he'd have expended many more words on his hiring spree. While I see this as the beginning of a pulp western series of books, it could easily compare to the pilot episode of a western TV show and those pilots usually run feature length for a reason: to allow for the necessary introductions. Unfortunately, each of the five key hires show up in chapters that mostly run a mere couple of pages each. I'd say that all of them are worthy of more substantial introductions.

And that's because that Ritter's choices are interesting, to say the very least. If they could be described as a little optimistic for the time, a secret team working one step away from the US President is the one place where social conventions could viably be ignored in favour of getting the job done. It also means that the sheer diversity of these recruits is something that would play well to future books. I presume that each member of the team will be given the spotlight in future stories in order to highlight precisely what makes them special to this unit. We start to see that here, but again we run out of pages before everyone gets a fair shot.

The other thing that stood out to me, ironically given the wild make-up of the X-Troop, is an attention to history. The United

States in 1876 is hardly my area of historical expertise, but, the X-Troop aside, this rings very true and there's a good use of period vocabulary to ground us in that setting. I left my review long enough that I can't remember which words I needed to look up, but there were a couple, whose meaning was still clear from context.

I'd recommend *The X-Troop* heartily to any-one who has an interest in pulp adventure and especially pulp westerns, though with the caveats that the layout may just drive you batty and there should have been a lot more pages than there were. There's an old theatre maxim that every performer should "leave them wanting more" and I'm eager for the next adventure of the X-Troop.

COLETTE BLACK

FOURTEEN

THE NUMBER PROPHECY #1

PUBLISHER:
DRAPUKAMO PUBLISHING

PUBLICATION DATE:
JULY 2015

I've been seeing promotional postcards for Colette Black's novels at many conventions for years, but somehow never managed to track down one of her books. So many authors, so little time! However, those cards kept her name in my mind and when I was given the opportunity to read a couple, I leapt at it.

Fourteen was something of a shock, because it doesn't feel like a self-published book and those of you who read enough of them will know just what a compliment that is. Sure, Drapukamo Publishing of Higley, AZ, doesn't seem to have a website of its own and there's the recognisable final page of a CreateSpace imprint, but the usual self-publishing problems are kept to a minimum. The use of smart-

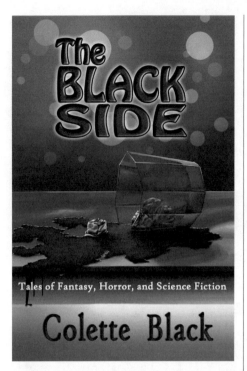

The plot is relatively simple: most of the book, the first volume in the *Number Prophecy* trilogy, is a chase scene, albeit one set in a complex and fantastic world with a feel for history and an eye for romance. Four characters are rather keen to get away from a fifth, as their lives depend on it, and they spend most of the book trying to do so. I presume the first sequel, titled *Thirteen* and due in mid-2016 (still outstanding), will slow their motion away and begin a very different journey back in.

The characters are well-delineated and also well-drawn, if somewhat predictably, and we cheer and boo accordingly. Their development is handled very well, but we know how they're going to change before they realise it themselves. While we do care about them and want to see that change happen, the plot revolves around danger and there just aren't enough characters to set up a George R. R. Martin environment where it doesn't matter if or how much we care, as the writer can kill them off anyway.

The villain is the all-powerful Emperor Beht Han, perhaps the ruler of his entire world, but he's by far the least interesting of the bunch because he's the standard Ming the Merciless type, which has never been sustainable. He's so utterly in control that the slightest deviation from his command or failure to achieve his goals can be, and usually is, punishable by instant death. He racks up quite a body count in three hundred pages. The only change he's likely to get will be his inevitable downfall, but I presume that's two books away. The story isn't about that eventuality, it's about what happens on the way to it.

quotes is inconsistent and there are a few odd typos and layout errors that should have been caught in proofing, but that's about it.

Instead, it has an original and stylish front cover and a good layout; it includes a couple of minor features that I'd like to figure out how to copy; and it's written in a comfortable writing style that suggests that there have been many million Colette Black words written before this book was ever begun. In fact, even with some flaws that I'll shortly go into, this is that rare self-published novel that could be easily sold to a major publisher. I could also see it adapted to film, as the majority of it is very cinematic indeed. Nominally young adult fiction, it's too edgy for Disney (when Disney start including nudity in films, I'll know I'm in the Twilight Zone) but it could play well in the right directorial hands and with the right sort of budget.

The most important character is the Fourteen of the title, so named because he's the fourteenth of the emperor's numerous children. That isn't a nod to Charlie Chan, it's a deliberate means to dehumanise them for reasons that we soon discover. In the early chapters, this focal point vies with three of his siblings to succeed him. However, succession isn't quite what they expect, the truth hinted at by the fact that the emperor's children are all sons physically identical to him, and when Fourteen discovers what's really going on, he rebels and runs, moving in one stroke from number fourteen son to public enemy number one.

Fourteen, or Gabrick, as his mother apparently named him before her own murder, has every bit of the story arc denied to the emperor. Sixteen years old, he's spent his entire life being trained and educated in the Numbers Compound, being readied for a potential ascension to the throne, but, as this life is the only one that he knows, he doesn't realise that he's been living in a luxurious prison. He aches to see the world beyond the walls, but finds the reality of it not remotely as comfortable as the one place to which he now can't return.

What's more, his sheltered upbringing also extends to people. Every person he's ever met is deferent, polite and subservient because, hey, he's the emperor's son. He has a servant of his own, the curvaceous Aednat, and he surreptitiously visits one of the Emperor's many concubines, Esterelle. It's no surprise that a man trained from birth to become an Emperor is full of self-importance, but going on the run is the biggest wake-up call he could ever get. Especially when it comes to people, the world outside doesn't remotely mimic what he's used to and he finds that his real education began the very moment he stepped beyond the walls.

Aednat is the second of the four running from the wrath of the emperor and she's the weakest of them by far, serving mostly (pun not intended) as a constant reminder of where Fourteen came from and what he's left behind. She exists primarily to highlight the changes in him as he experiences the world and finds that what he always wanted isn't necessarily what he wants now.

Smitten with Aednat, he wouldn't suggest that he wants Mariessa, but it's pretty obvious from the outset that they're going to end up together. Her story starts with her violent sale into slavery to become one of the Emperor's mothers, one who will give birth to one of those identical sons. As the voice of rebellion in the story, she resists immediately and, somewhat like a feral creature, continues to resist throughout. She grows as well, realising

57

that some people are the way they are because it's all they know and that it is possible for them to change of their own accord. She also finds that she changes more than anyone else, after discovering that she's of sorceress stock and her small body contains a vast power.

If Mariessa has grounding in a world that's unfathomable to Fourteen, Master Chid Den, professional man of danger, has even more. While he may be the closest thing to a friend that the emperor has ever had, that's no friend at all, and he patiently waits for his opportunity to take him down. He sees it in Fourteen, his young student, so whisks him away from his fate at the emperor's hands to freedom in the world outside and we gradually realise that his act has the potential to fulfill a prophecy. It also helps that he's also protective of Aednat, in a fatherly way. Mariessa is the only wildcard to him.

If these are decent, if not too surprising, characters, the greatest success of this book is that they're thrown into a fascinating world. Colette Black never tells us whether this is an alien planet or an alternate Earth, but it's an eerily familiar place, crafted out of Chinese culture, colonial arrogance, the Indian caste system and a host of other very Earthly influences. While I do want to follow Fourteen's destined journey and see how it all plays out, I especially want to discover more about the world that Black created here.

Society is strictly structured, with every human being except the Numbers, belonging to a tier which reflects their status. As that tier is tattooed onto them soon after birth for the world to see, movement between the many classes is hardly commonplace. Growing up in the sheltered Numbers Compound, Fourteen never saw a single soul below tier five, who were the servants. Yet, outside the palace, he discovers that the world is full of people occupying tiers as low as ten and that, well, they're people too. His inherent arrogance is constantly checked by the reality he experiences and it's fascinating to watch it broken.

It's not difficult to see that such a ruthless authoritarian system is ripe for the tumbling (isn't that what they have to do in prophecy trilogies?), but it's highly refreshing to see such care and attention devoted to the art of worldbuilding as we move towards that eventuality. *Fourteen* runs over three hundred pages in length, but it focuses almost entirely on a quartet of characters, with the emperor an omnipresent threat to them all and a few others waiting in the wings for a moment or two of their own. The real supporting character, though, is the world of Dixho itself and I look forward to watching it grow over the next two books in the trilogy.

I enjoyed *Fourteen* a great deal, even if it was less for its story and more for its world and the writing of Colette Black. I'll certainly look for *Thirteen*, when it's published, and wonder about the title of the third and last book in the trilogy.

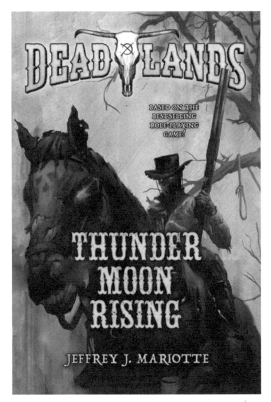

JEFFREY J. MARIOTTE

THUNDER MOON RISING

DEADLANDS #1

PUBLISHER:
TOR

PUBLICATION DATE:
APRIL 2014

I mentioned in my review of *Ghostwalkers*, the first of three novels from Tor to tie in to the *Deadlands* role-playing game, that author Jonathan Maberry had set a high standard for his succeeding authors to follow. I am very happy to report that Jeff Mariotte rose to that challenge and delivered another glorious romp into the weird west. Next up will be Seanan McGuire's contribution to wrap up the set. I do hope that the three books will find enough success to prompt Tor to commission more.

I should add that these books don't follow on from each other; they merely share a universe. For those coming in fresh with book two, which is a perfectly valid approach to take, *Deadlands* takes the wild west that we know and shakes it up a little, quite literally as a matter of fact, as half of California is now underwater, sheared off by the big one of 1868. Rather than taking a quintessentially steampunk approach to advance the period's technology with ever more intricate clockwork and steam power, a mysterious mineral called ghost rock has been exposed and it powers things like nothing else.

Ghostwalkers focused strongly on ghost rock, which also has the unfortunate side effect of raising the dead, but Mariotte curiously avoids it in *Thunder Moon Rising* in favour of a rather different source for monsters. And monsters there are, even if we wonder for quite some time whether we'll get to meet any for more than a moment.One does show his face early on, right after murdering a whore named Daisie upstairs at Senora Soto's saloon and

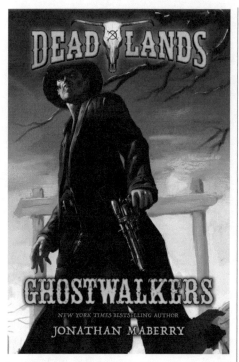

and the nearby Fort Huachuca. As deeply as he delves into these characters, he never forgets that there's a lead, who is inexorably dragged through the story by the power of art. If a protagonist makes things happen, Tuck isn't one of those because things happen to him a heck of a lot more than he happens to them.

I'd have to go back to *Ghostwalkers* to make a proper comparison, but it felt like Maberry's story was a little more involved, albeit still threadbare for a four hundred page tome, while Mariotte's characterisations are deeper and more satisfying. Their respective leads have so much in common that I'd be hard pressed if I had to choose between them: just as Maberry's haunted gunfighter, Grey Torrance, has to deal not only with the supernatural threat in front of him but with the one rising up out of his past, so does Mariotte's Tuck Bringloe have to deal with his own demons as much as the ones that array against him. However, I only remember a few key players in *Ghostwalkers*, while I remember a whole host of them in *Thunder Moon Rising*. It merely takes a while for the key players to emerge from their peers and for their strands of plot to merge.

brothel, but he promptly vanishes into the night, leaving only Tucker Bringloe, the resident drunk in the southern Arizona town of Carmichael, with a good look at his inhuman visage. Well, Tucker and us, because that's surely him on the front cover in the absolutely stunning painting by Aaron J. Riley. Town Marshal Turville rounds up a posse, of course, which he insists Bringloe join, and they all head off in hot pursuit. What's odd is that we stay in hot pursuit for much longer than we might expect.

Mariotte follows Maberry's lead in a number of regards. He knows he has a lot of pages to fill so he takes his time, exercising a great deal of patience as he explores a variety of characters with admirable depth. However he also keeps his actual story very simple, leaving the complexity for the people of Carmichael and those occupying its surround-ing ranches

If there's a real complaint to be made against Mariotte, it's that this weird west yarn doesn't seem weird enough for far too long. It gets there, trust me, but it remains a western with eventual weirdness rather than the thoroughly weird west story we might expect. At least the weirdness is the canvas on which the western is painted, but the painting always covers the canvas and things of darkness only creep through at the most important of moments.

And with a complaint made, I'll follow that up with a compliment. Mariotte knows southern Arizona well and he brings the Huachuca mountains and the surrounding area capably to life. This is a big state and it had a lot fewer people in it back then when it was only a territory. Mariotte gives us the town of Carmichael, some ranches and a fort but, more overtly, he gives us the impression of space; small town life might seem big to people living it, but it starts to feel acutely exposed when the supernatural comes knocking on our door. Sure, there's Tombstone but that's a long way away and it's not that big either. I really appreciated the way the tough guys of the west became rather vulnerable when the teeth of the story are eventually exposed

I've read a few of Jeff Mariotte's novels and this is easily the biggest and best of them. Given that I've seen him at so many of our local events, I have a bunch more sitting on my shelf ready to go and this makes me want to leap into them soon. Sure, I'd have appreciated a more complex plot to match its complex characters, but I'll happily take the latter over neither.

Beyond Tuck Bringloe, who has a peach of a story arc, I honestly had little idea which of the cast of characters would become prominent and which would be ruthlessly killed off. I've been told by a number of authors that every single character is the lead of their own story and they should be written that way. Mariotte does a fantastic job of doing that here, because even his minor characters are drawn well enough to invite us into their lives. It felt notable when they died and it felt important when those with a higher purpose met each other.

There are other things that I want to highlight because they especially impressed me, but they tended to come late in the book and any attempt to describe them would fall into spoiler territory. Let's just say that many of them are locations, which are constructed with a cinematic eye rather than a painter's. They breathe and move and resonate. There's a ranch house, for instance, that I would dearly love to see filmed, even before things start to happen there and those would just add to the glory of it.

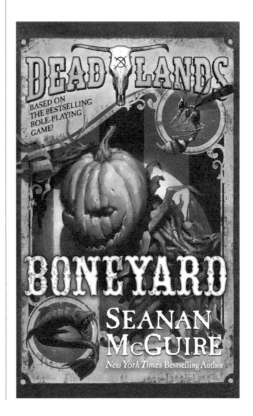

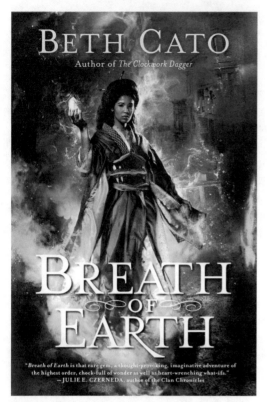

BETH CATO

BREATH OF EARTH

INGRID CARMICHAEL #1

PUBLISHER:
HARPERVOYAGER
PUBLICATION DATE:
AUGUST 2016

I liked Beth Cato's first book, *The Clockwork Dagger*, which was nominated for the Locus Award for Best First Novel. I liked its sequel, *The Clockwork Crown*, even more, because it addressed all my minor issues with the first book and kicked everything that was good about it into high gear. Her third book, which is unrelated to the previous two, is a step up again. I adored *Breath of Earth* from beginning to end and am upset only at how long I'll have to wait before I can devour the inevitable sequel, because this is just a beginning.

Those two books are steampunk fantasies, set in an imaginary world with imaginary geography, imaginary history and imaginary characters. This one is still mostly imaginary but it seems a heck of a lot more familiar, because it unfolds in San Francisco, albeit an alternate one that's a little different to what we've read about, because of the fantasy element and some engaging alternate history.

It's 1906 (yes, we know what happened in our San Francisco in 1906; you're leaping ahead) and the city is part of the Unified Pacific, an alliance of the United States and Japan, the latter of which have shaped the culture, fashion and even healthcare of the former to a major degree. The current enemy is China, who are losing hard. Britannia is tied up with a resurgence of the Thuggee Cult (and those who benefit from such a thing) in India. Russia and the Ottoman Empire are also major players who are merely far enough abstracted to not affect this particular book.

Magic is real, in the form of geomancers who absorb energy from the ground and channel it into a mineral called kermanite, which is then used to power anything that needs it, such as the abundant airships which mark the only real nod to steampunk here. The ground moves because of massive creatures underneath it called Hidden Ones who toss and turn over time. Other folklore elements crop up here and there, sometimes in a major way, and will surely play a bigger part yet in future books.

However, this magic is grounded, pun not intended, and Beth Cato does her level best to keep it all consistent and explore the ramifications of its application just as if folklore were science. Clearly San Francisco is in need of a gaggle of geomancers to keep itself stable, so what would happen if their building, the Earth Wardens Cordilleran Auxiliary, just happened to be destroyed in mysterious fashion with all its protectors inside? Who would do such a thing and what would it mean to the city at large, especially in 1906 (yes, welcome back, you anticipators, you)? And more sinister still, what if there were a means to turn geomancy itself into a weapon? How much damage could that cause?

There's a great deal of mystery here and perhaps the biggest success of the novel is how capably Cato builds it. She introduces this San Francisco well and I felt that I understood it as she placed me into it, but my knowledge grew with the page count, just as it does for the lead character, Ingrid Carmichael. She's the secretary of Warden Takaguchi, also a father figure for her since the disappearance of her own and the only one who knows what she's actually capable of. She learns too, because events overtake her and throw her into a lot more adventure than she could ever have imagined.

Another success here is in Cato's choice of characters. This 1906 is a sexist, misogynistic place, as indeed was the real 1906, and that mindset pervades the world for someone as capable as Ingrid. However, it's also a notably racist place, especially against the opposing Chinese, relegated in this California to Chinatowns ruled by the tongs. The Japanese are friends and allies, as are the Hawaiians (their nation run here by the Japanese rather than the Americans), but native languages and cultures are suppressed and authorities are quick to react.

I'd love to talk more about the companions Ingrid falls in with after she escapes from the Auxiliary explosion, but that way lies massive spoilers. Suffice it to say that each character who bands together with her is hiding an important secret about who they are, though not necessarily in any of the ways that you might expect. Cato deserves great praise for writing characters like these and I'm sure that she'll receive that for one in particular (hey, Fenris, we're talking about you), not only because of the careful choices she made in doing so but because she made them intelligently enough that they simply don't appear to be worthy of mention and thus are, all the more.

If I can't really talk about Ingrid, Cy, Fenris and Lee without revealing spoilers, I can at least say that I appreciated all of them a great deal. Instead I'll mention how I was less appreciative of Captain Sutcliff, who appears to be just as carefully insubstantial as the others are engaging. As a headstrong officer of the American Army & Airship Corps, he may well have his secrets too, but they're not explored here. He's merely an annoyance, someone good at getting in the way and getting the wrong end of the stick, often at the same time. I'm not sure whether he himself or the force that he represents should have been more substantial, but it's one or the other. Maybe future books in the series will expand on how authority works in the Unified Pacific because, Captain Sutcliff aside, I'm sure it does, even if we don't see it much here.

I can also mention a character who doesn't actually appear but does come up a lot in the narrative. He's Teddy Roosevelt, who in this world isn't the US President but an Ambassador, one of twelve who sit above the leadership of the allied nations and wield great power. We do get to meet a different Ambassador and I'll keep my mouth shut there too, but surely Roosevelt is going to live up to the potential of his character in further novels.

If it feels like I haven't said much about the substance within 'Breath of Earth', it's because it's wrapped up either in the lead characters or the complex sociopolitical background that underpins what happens. I can't talk about the former because I'd spoil what should be a host of discoveries for you. I shouldn't talk about the latter because that would be boring out of the context of those discoveries. Both could easily prompt long essays, if not theses, and I'm sure that someone will write them for your edification and enjoyment after you've read this book.

And, yes, you should read this. Just ponder on what's here Alternate history. Grounded fantasy. Politics and intrigue. Adventure and airships. A unique magic system. Traditional folklore. Cross-pollination of cultures. Oh yes, you should read it. It's rather like a checklist of all the things that should be in a modern fantasy novel that doesn't want to do what all those other modern fantasy novels are doing.

Unfortunately, having read this before its official release date, I'm stuck with a long wait indeed before I can read a sequel. Maybe I should build a habit of breaking into Cato's house at night, stealing the cookies out of her fridge and sneaking a read of her work in progress. Hey, I can blame it on kitsune, right?

BETH CATO

BREATH OF EARTH

INGRID CARMICHAEL #2

PUBLISHER:
HARPERVOYAGER
PUBLICATION DATE:
AUGUST 2017

It's been a long while since I've looked forward to a book as much as this one and I'm happy to say that it delivers. Its most obvious flaw isn't its own fault, as it's inherently a middle book, building on what went before (in the fantastic *Breath of Earth*, which I eagerly re-read before diving into this one) and setting up what is yet to come (in at least one more novel; Ingrid Carmichael's story feels like it will end up as a trilogy but could well become a series). Outside of that, it's a thoroughly enjoyable work of fantasy and a highly worthy sequel.

In *Breath of Earth*, Cato created a glorious alternate world. She conjured it out of known historical fact but made a number of changes to what we know in our reality: Japan, rather than the United States, invaded Hawaii and the two nations forged a political alliance called the United Pacific. She extrapolated how that would change the culture of North America, not just in costume and manners but also by superstition and folklore shaping the culture and technology. She also confirms that this folklore isn't just make-believe. There are both reiki practitioners manipulating energy and Pasteurian doctors keen on clean; both of them work, even if it's in different ways. There are characters, whether "human", "animal" or "spirit", who are creatures clipped from exotic mythologies.

What's more, earthquakes in this world are caused by Hidden Ones, underground kaiju who are merely turning over in their sleep. Best of all, these earthquakes can be countered by geomancers taking in the energy, which they, in turn, project into a mineral called kermanite, which is then used to power airships and other machines. Cato certainly handled her worldbuilding carefully, neatly extrapolating each of her little exceptions to our reality to generate a fantastic and internally consistent background against which her stories can unfold.

And I have to be careful here, because all her central characters are keeping big secrets. While some of them were exposed in *Breath of Earth*, you shouldn't know about them until you read that book.

I'll go as far as to talk a little about Ingrid Carmichael because the back cover blurb does a bunch of that and, if HarperVoyager don't consider it a spoiler, then I certainly can't. Ingrid's a geomancer of immense power, but most people don't know that because she's a girl and an exotic one at that, that "exotic" here meaning of mixed heritage and thus not quite the same colour as everyone else. She learned a lot about who she is by the end of *Breath of Earth*, which ended with an earthquake destroying the city of San Francisco and her fleeing the city in a small but fast airship called the *Palmetto Bug* with her old friend Lee and a pair of newfound compatriots, Cy and Fenris.

I won't, however, tell you a bunch of other things. I won't tell you what Ingrid learned, because that's an ongoing process and it gets pretty serious in *Call of Fire*. I won't tell you the secret Lee's keeping, but I'll note that Ingrid finds herself tied up in his story far more than she ever expected, courtesy of a cool creature from folklore that takes a shine to her. Oh, and it joyously isn't the only one! I won't tell you what Fenris is hiding, because that really isn't important and I'm still incredibly happy that

it's treated that way here even more than it was in the first book. And I won't tell you Cy's secret either, except to say that what he has hidden from others is mirrored in what others have hidden from him, things which will no doubt be a major part of book three. How's that for a bunch of vague hints as to what might be going on here?

This ragtag bunch of misfits fly north from the wreckage of San Francisco to the city of Portland, to seek out United Pacific Ambassador Theodore Roosevelt. Yes, that one. While he was referenced in *Breath of Earth*, he actually shows up here and he's quite a lot of fun in a much more realistic way than I had expected, a driven character who's not drawn either black or white. Eventually, they have to move further north, to Seattle, and even more things happen there. There's an escalation in play that seems to kick in with each city on Ingrid's itinerary.

But back to Portland. I love the way that Cato sets up what our players do in Portland. Initially, we have a woman of colour, for that's really what Ingrid is, even if that colour isn't quite as dark as it would usually be for such a description, and a Chinese youth passing as Japanese (which is a huge deal when the the latter are allies but the former are the enemy), wandering together into Portland's Chinatown which is already on fire when they arrive. And things only get more complicated from there! Race is a big deal in these books, but not just where it seems to be; the conflict building between the United Pacific and the remnants of China often overshadows the fact that our heroine isn't the usual white girl we might take her for.

We learn a lot more in this book than its predecessor, suggesting that *Breath of Earth* was mostly about setting a stage and putting the cast of characters into motion; *Call of Fire* is where we find out what and how and why, amidst growing tension; and the next volume will presumably be how it all wraps up. Lots of questions are answered here, though far from all of them. On a personal level, both Ingrid and Cy get news of family that they utterly weren't expecting, while, on a grand political level, they start to understand the plans of the people who are manipulating everything on a global scale.

Cato isn't willing for them to figure everything out, though, and she's more than happy to throw them a curveball or three. I particularly enjoyed how they decide to leave for Seattle just at the time that gold is discovered in the far north and the ensuing riot frustrates their attempts. Of course, that announcement is as much a coincidence as your cynical mind suspects, which is to say it's all very much part of a clever plan. There are quite a few plans in operation here and I'm eager to see how they play out. If I'm guessing correctly, Cato will take the obvious road on a grand scale but really mix it up as she does so, surprising us with the details. I'm eager to see if that's true or not.

And so, while I can't talk about most of what I want to talk about, I can happily report that there's a great deal of good here. The characters are even more deeply defined than before. The action is intense, on the macro and micro scales. The political intrigue, which is truly long-reaching, was far from clear in *Breath of Earth* but is enticingly explored here. Perhaps what I like best about this series is how Cato is able to play with such a fascinating variety of fantasy elements but ground them all in what seems like a completely rational world. How Ingrid interacts with what are called "fantastics" here, those creatures of folklore, is fantasy through and through, but Cato grounds it in a neat conversation about how language changes, covering native tales, missionary translations and contemporary understanding.

Call of Fire is Beth Cato's fourth novel and it's the first to not notably improve on the last. I was rather scared of that progression, given how *Breath of Fire* was the best book I read last year. I'd suggest that this isn't quite up to its standards, but it truly would be unfair to say that until I've read the next book in Ingrid Carmichael's story and I can see how everything flows between the volumes. For now, I'll have to restrict myself to saying that this is a thoroughly enjoyable sequel that inherently suffers a little by not being the beginning or the end. Bring on book three!

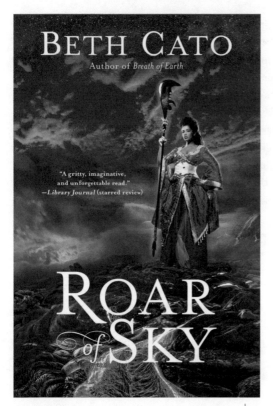

BETH CATO

ROAR OF SKY

INGRID CARMICHAEL #3

PUBLISHER:
HARPERVOYAGER

PUBLICATION DATE:
OCTOBER 2018

I've been disappointed by a number of final volumes in trilogies lately, so I'm happy to say that Beth Cato is bucking that trend and I'm not just saying that because my Nameless Zine review of the previous volume, *Call of Fire*, is quoted in the praise section at the beginning of this one.

There's a heck of a lot to like here, even if this volume brings a few less surprises than its predecessors; it is an ending, after all. That "heck of a lot" is also so evenly spread that I'm hard pressed to say what I liked most.

I've loved Cato's worldbuilding throughout the trilogy and that continues here. For those new to the series (and, yes, you should certainly read in order), we start out in *Breath of Earth* in an alternate 1906 San Francisco, just before the big quake that we remember from our history. What's different in this alternate history is that quakes are caused by motion of Hidden Ones, gigantic creatures of legend who live within the earth, and the energy that's generated by their movement can be safely shifted, by the talents of geomancers, into the mineral kermanite; which, when so infused with energy, is used to power the airships and machines of this fantastic world.

There's a lot there to be going along with, but there's more to consider. Here, the United States is a partner with Imperial Japan in a political alliance called the United Pacific, so there's a strong Japanese influence woven into the North America in which all this action and intrigue unfolds. Some of that is undeniably positive, some more neutral and some particularly negative, such as the growing racism against the Chinese, against which our core story develops. You see, the balance of power between the US and Japan within the United Pacific is shifting, deliberately so according to the plans of the villain of the piece, who I won't name, even if the back cover blurb does. I'd see that as a spoiler.

By this point, the series has already taken us from San Francisco to Seattle. Here it moves us on to Hawaii, the ancestral home of our lead character, Ingrid Carmichael, who doesn't remotely have the family tree that her name might suggest. She's eager to meet her grandmother, who I also won't name, but, in doing so, she finds both more and less than she expects. This meeting between generations is a great example of how Cato is adept at merging reality with fantasy, which is one of my favourite aspects in these books.

Another is the way in which she writes characters who are diverse without ever being preachy. Ingrid is not my colour, my race, my nationality or my gender, and her story takes place two-thirds of a century before I was born in an alternate history that isn't mine, but I had no problems at all understanding what makes her tick or empathising with her. What's more, there are reasons why she is who she is, none of which feel awkward or contrived. As she begins this book, Ingrid is also disabled, having damaged herself in the events of the previous book, and that change drives so much of what unfolds here. Again, there are reasons, and none have anything to do with checkboxes. In fact, there's a notably bittersweet section where Ingrid finds herself yet again the victim of racism but in a fashion that acknowledges her real race for the first time. There are layers here. And yes, I'm also happy to report that the notable reveal in the first book is let entirely be as the trilogy wraps up, which approach is much appreciated; any attempt to leverage it for plot purposes would have cheapened the trilogy and Cato resists the urge.

She also does a fantastic job of exploring details. Ingrid now has difficulty walking, so she spends a good deal of her time in a wheelchair. That's about as obvious a consequence as they come but some writers would have stopped there; Cato is aware that she can't just stop there when she's placing that wheelchair into Japanese-administered Hawaii in her alternate 1906. She doesn't magic up wheelchair ramps; she explores the reality of her fantasy instead. To highlight another, less quantifiable example, I appreciated the idea of moulting sylph fluff being seen as a hazard to airship ventilation. It's not an important plot point and it only warrants a brief mention but it's a problem that our characters have to face and it does a magnificent job of making their wild and incredible world a believable one for us. It grounds it as much as some of Cato's historical research does.

Now, Cato does play fast and loose with a few historical elements, but that's her right as an author. I enjoyed the trip to a nickel theater anyway, even if it's a little more sophisticated than it should be for 1906. It felt right in context and she doesn't make the common error of assuming that theatres were silent just because they showed silent films. I even learned something here, about the role of the benshi in Japanese silent theaters. The point here is that time and place is gloriously established, even when Cato doesn't adhere to the minutiae of the era.

Talking of film, I was absolutely thrilled to read what is clearly an homage to the Miles

Brothers' short film, *A Trip Down Market Street Before the Fire*, which is one of the most important actuality films ever made, depicting as it does the San Francisco that existed only a few days before it was destroyed in the 1906 earthquake and ensuing fire. Here, Cato echoes it in newsreel footage taken after the earthquake, with an intertitle reading, "San Francisco. We remember. We mourn." I was blissful afterwards when the author pointed out to me that there is indeed a follow-up actuality, presumably made by other hands, and I had a blast comparing the two films later, made so close together in the same place but so utterly and devastatingly different.

There are downsides, albeit minor ones. While many of the positive attributes of the first two books continue, the gradual wrapping up of a number of plot strands makes this one seem more inevitable and predictable. I have absolutely no idea, of course, how Cato could have avoided that without a groundbreaking twist that would probably have felt wrong; I think it's just inherent when a third volume has to wrap up a story with this much momentum going into it.

I was surprised to find the *Excalibur*, a vast flying weapons facility which threatened so much in foreshadowing, turn out to be rather underwhelming, but I think it's mostly due to this steampunk Death Star not getting to do much except looking ominous. To be fair, the comparisons don't run too closely, so there's a lot more originality here than it might seem, and Cato successfully avoids all the clichés, especially the usual convenient flaw, replaced here by something suitably horrifying that resonates well both in our time and with a neat nod to a Victorian classic in the process.

Those are minor flaws that don't cause any

damage to the trilogy. The one flaw that does is the way in which many of the supporting characters fade away disappointingly.

While the series was always going to revolve around Ingrid Carmichael, there are other characters who stood their ground with her or against her throughout the first two books on their own merits, but here they adopted more simple roles of mere sidekicks and villains. It certainly isn't all of them (and one such minor character makes a surprising return to expand magnificently), but it does include some of the most prominent ones and I wonder whether Cato will return to some of them in the future in side stories. It isn't on her radar now, as she's moving onto an enticing new idea that I can't mention, but it seems to me that there are easy openings to make a return to this world, if she ever feels the need, even though Ingrid's story is now told.

All in all, I've been thoroughly entertained by this trilogy and it's one to which I plan to return. I did expect to say that about a few others recently, but their final volumes were underwhelming and lessened what had gone before. While it could easily be argued that *Roar of Sky* is the weakest of the three Ingrid Carmichael books, there's still much in it to recommend and it doesn't lessen her story.

This trilogy is original, engaging and told with the sort of voice that many aim for and precious few achieve. It's also a great example of a work of period fantasy that raises many questions about our current reality without ever sermonising. Yes, writers, stories can be told about characters of other ethnicities, nationalities, ages, genders, races, sexualities, etc. and still be damn good stories, without any need on our behalf to question their authors' political leanings.

JOHN PAUL RIED

RECKLESS AMBITIONS

THE MEDFORD FAMILY CHRONICLES #1

PUBLISHER:
AZ PUBLISHING SERVICES

PUBLICATION DATE:
FEBRUARY 2016

There's a maxim used by authors that says that you should never base a fantasy novel on a roleplaying campaign. But why? After all, dungeon masters have to create in a similar way to writers of fantasy novels, with similar skills needed in character creation and world building. Well, here's a textbook example to discuss, because author John Paul Ried is an avid gamer, an experienced dungeon master and now the author of three books in what promises to be an ongoing series of fantasy novels, which he freely admits are set in a world that he built for AD&D campaigns. And, had I not known that because I happen to have chatted with John about it or because I read the acknowledgements before the novel, it's completely obvious nonetheless.

All the good here comes out of the creative juices that are shared by DMs and authors, most obviously their strong vision of world building. Ried clearly knows the land of Palamar just like it's his own back yard and he can visualise it as he sets each of his characters about their business within it. He also knows those characters well, having inhabited their skins or directed their actions. In particular, he's played Oliver Wendell Enalan personally in campaigns and, looking at story arcs, that's hardly surprising either.

All the bad here comes out of the differences between games and novels. In a game, everything has to be oriented around rules, goals and decisions, because that's how things work. Rules are set to define what's possible or impossible, goals are set to guide the players and decisions determine how they can move.

Novels need rules too but each character also needs a goal, not just those being played, and decisions can have much more subtle effects than are usually the case in a game. That especially applies when those decisions are about life or death.

I enjoyed this novel, but I enjoyed it because of the passion that was clearly poured into it. Ried is a man with a twinkle in his eye and he's obviously having a blast letting these stories flow out of his virtual pen onto the printed page. That passion is contagious and I often found myself grinning while reading. That isn't to say that I didn't have a whole slew of problems with this book but we'll get into that soon enough.

At heart, this is a game of thrones, because everything thus far revolves around the battle for the Ruby Throne of the Palamaran Empire, which sits at the heart of Paladon City. The

much respected Emperor John Cardillion III has died, after a long and successful reign, but his talents at running an empire clearly didn't extend to his family, as his four sons promptly fall to bickering about the succession. Each is willing, even eager, to wage war to claim what they believe can only be theirs, everyone and everything else be damned, and the Medford family finds itself stuck in the middle. They're obviously the focus because, as much as Ried talks about the Palamaran Adventures, the label on the front of the book is the Medford Family Chronicles.

There are two key Medfords as we begin. One is Thomas Wilson Oakley, Earl of Medford, Lord Chancellor of the Council of Earls and Supreme Commander of the Imperial Guard Legion. The other is his eighteen year old daughter, Lady Christina Cecilia Medford, whose beauty he plans to marry off to whichever Cardillion son manages to seize the throne.

In gaming terms, these four sons are respectively a cleric, a warrior, a mage and a thief, each of whom is drawn almost entirely from one easily delineated characteristic.

Prince Philip Canalon Cardillion is first to act. He's the thief, a successful businessman in Paladon City, who plans to seize the throne through fraud, promises and bribes, not to ignore a prompt assassination attempt against Lord Medford so as to take the Imperial Guard. It fails, of course, and Medford sends in the Guard to forcefully arrest him, then raid his estate for valuables and burn it to the ground.

Arch Cleric Samalek serves the Fire God Zemelon, whose compound is in Paladon City. He's a religious fanatic who is more than ready to kickstart a holy war to purge the empire of magic and heresy. Medford sets up this cult as the destroyers of Canalon's estate and has its leadership arrested for treason. His goal is to prompt a riot, which the Guard will suppress, leaving a second faction weakened.

Field Marshal David Nordan, the warrior, is a brutal and militaristic leader who withdraws his armies from the war that they're already fighting so that they can fight his instead; they march on Paladon City with the aim of sacking it and taking the throne by force. At this point, we wonder what "brutal and militaristic" will mean, after seeing what Medford has already got up to with Canalon and Samalek.

Finally, there's Wizard Baron Richard Lothar Cardillion, a powerful mage at Gamemasters University, an institution dedicated to exploring all parallel dimensions for new games to play. Under the leadership of its headmaster Thedkhan Utas, they all leave Paladon City for the province of Senaria, as it secedes from the empire, with the goal of returning once everything has calmed down.

As you can tell, there's not a lot of subtlety here. Ried focuses in on a turbulent moment in time and sets a batch of archetypes at each other's throats with a city and an empire as their backdrop. This is a lot of fun on a macro scale. It's also a lot of fun at the micro scale because these larger than life characters are busy folk who never seem to do anything that isn't eventful. There are many more than just those I've mentioned, as Ried's cast of characters is expansive and many of them get their turns in the spotlight.

For instance, Oliver Wendell Enalan, the character with whom Ried identifies in his acknowledgements, has connections to many different subplots and grows substantially, from a minor wizard who drinks at the Drunken Kitty Kat Tavern to... well, you'll have to read on, but Ried does spoil part of that

discovery by listing the discovery of "latent psionic abilities" in the back cover blurb. I enjoyed Enalan a lot, because he has a lot more opportunity than more important characters stuck playing the roles given to them. He can grow and he does. Other favourite characters do likewise. Many don't.

Unfortunately, most of those eventful moments don't stand up to much scrutiny. In a game, that's fine as we make our decisions, experience the ramifications and move on. In a novel, there's a need for more care in the details to make sure that everything holds up and remains consistent.

For instance, there's a point where a highly talented nine year old does something important and so is recognised for his deeds. No problem there, but he's promptly given a suit of armour that fits him like a glove. Now, do they keep suits of armour on the rack for nine year olds in Paladon City or do they just construct them overnight? The big picture here is great, emotional and rewarding. The little picture makes no sense at all.

And that happens a lot. Never mind nine year olds, every time anyone does anything remotely notable in this book, they're immediately promoted. We often don't see who was in the positions they've just taken over, as that's not important; only the promotions are. Our heroes seem to be as bloodthirsty as those they claim moral superiority over; apparently it's fine to kill, burn and loot, as long as you're on the side of the good guys. The palace's secret passages really can't be deemed secret when everyone and their dog is rampaging through them. And, of course, the Gamemasters University is a great idea for a game but it's really difficult to figure out how it actually works within the pages of a novel.

And much of the problem here comes back to that maxim about not writing fantasy novels based on RPG campaigns. While they do share some of the same needs, they differ on others. Characters have feelings and can't just be manoeuvred through a set of situations without things changing. When one character is raped, it doesn't matter that the rape was interrupted and the rapist killed; it matters that she was raped and she's not going to go talking about it to a crowded room the very next day.

I'll happily continue reading this series as I'm enjoying Ried's big and bold world, but in large part also because I'm interested in seeing how things change as he finds his feet as an novelist as a separate role to a DM.

JOHN PAUL RIED

CAPRICIOUS DEITIES

THE MEDFORD FAMILY CHRONICLES #2

PUBLISHER:
AZ PUBLISHING SERVICES

PUBLICATION DATE:
MAY 2016

My review of *Reckless Ambitions*, the first book by local author John Paul Ried, in his *Medford Family Chronicles* fantasy series, was an awkward one to craft because Ried wrote a thoroughly enjoyable novel while falling into many of the pitfalls that lie in wait for wannabe writers. It won out because of his clear passion for his characters and the world they inhabit, but it was still riddled with plot conveniences, wild leaps and crazy inconsistencies. I wanted to read more but have to admit that I was wary, too.

I'm happy to say that *Capricious Deities*, the second volume in this series, is much better written than its predecessor and without most of that book's problems. In fact, it's a much better book in every way I can think of.

I believe that Ried, who conjured these novels out of a long-running AD&D campaign, wanted so badly to take a world that he created for gaming (and which many had clearly enjoyed) and give it a second life in fiction that he shoehorned far too much into that first volume. I might argue that he cared a great deal more about the world of the Palamaran Empire than he did about framing a coherent story within it. It was an introduction to a broad swathe of characters, races and locations, many of whom have their own stories that were merely hinted at as asides. The title of that book could easily refer to the reckless abandon with which Ried threw himself into that project.

Capricious Deities, on the other hand, calms things down a great deal. Instead of the beginnings of many stories, some of which we'll never hear, which unfold on the sidelines while we wait for Thomas Medford to get round to taking the one and only option really available to him, namely to claim the Ruby Throne and rule the Palamaran Empire himself, Ried focuses in almost entirely on a single story, namely the civil war that erupted after the untimely death of Emperor John Cardillion III, Thomas's predecessor and the father of four idiots with more balls than brains.

One of those four sons died in the first book. Two more have combined forces and plan to march north to sack Paladon City and seize the throne. The fourth is mostly absent. And so, if the first book was an AD&D game of thrones, this second is a wargame, with two vast armies moving towards each other for an inevitable scrap. And, for all the mistakes that Ried made

in his first book, he nails a more difficult challenge in the second, which is to let a big story unfold on its own while person-ifying it through the little stories of people caught up in it. Many authors have come a cropper on that one and Ried doesn't join their company.

Some of the characters continue on from *Reckless Ambitions*, the most obvious being Nicholas Armand, an able soldier whose rank I'll avoid mentioning because it changes every dozen pages. He's thrown right in at the deep end by Emperor Thomas, who has finally discovered that Nick has been carrying on with his daughter, Lady Christina Medford. So, off to war he goes, initially unaware that the army's commander has been ordered by the emperor to ensure his glorious death in battle. That commander is another prominent character from book one, Paul Tenisal, an Earl and now a Field Marshal, who has other secrets to share too.

On the other side, there are two of the former emperor's four sons, Prince Philip Canalon and Arch Cleric Samalek, the thief and the cleric. One of the reasons that we never doubt which side is going to win this war is that these two are given much less development than their opposite numbers. They're cardboard cutout villains, merely of different villainous archetypes, while we gain some real insight into Armand and Tenisal. In fact, they're not even the people to fear, that role going to the Fire God Zemelon, who does show up here in person to wreak his havoc on the battlefield. I loved those scenes and have respect for Ried not just for writing them but for writing them in the way that he did.

Other characters we know pop in and out, especially during the bookends that set up the war and follow it, especially Oliver Wendell

Enalan, professor at the Gamemasters University and obvious avatar for Ried himself. As before, he's a heck of a lot of fun, but he's growing so quickly and so strongly that we do wonder how much room he's got to continue on that path. Given that this book involves a number of gods, I'm half expecting him to join their number sooner rather than later.

Many characters are new, though, and I appreciated that. I also appreciated that they mostly weren't folk invested in one side or other of the war which threatens to engulf their home of Grabinth Hollow. Instead, they are simply folk who got caught up in the war only because it threatens to engulf their town and them along with it. This is a fantastic approach and Ried handles it well before, during and after the bloodshed.

Even where Ried includes subplots that don't pertain directly to the war, their inclusion makes sense, in another improvement from the first book where Ried threw everything he could at the wall to see what would stick; here he knows what to throw and he targets it all much better. So, we set up some conflict between Emperor Thomas and his daughter Christina, which is well played even if it's never as tense as Ried wants it to be. We set the stage for book three with the arrival of new races in Palamar City in the form of a gargoyle ambassador, Gargameleche, and his ogre crew, looking for the elves whom we met in book one. We even identify a fiancé for young hero Neshal who shares his massive potential.

So, much of the success of this book revolves around Ried ditching all the things that didn't work in the previous one, while focusing in on a single story and telling it well. The rest of its success lies on the one thing that he

didn't ditch from the first book, which is its life. Ried lives for this stuff and I'm convinced that if he could wave a wand and transport himself to Palamar, he would. He cares about this world and everything in it, from its people to its politics. He expounds on everything about it with a passion that is palpable.

What's more, that passion is refreshing not only for its depth but for its breadth. Ried's stories are told with glee, even when they revolve around murder, torture and deicide; many of the good guys, right up to Emperor Thomas, are not good guys in the slightest; they're just clearly a better choice than the bad guys. And, while this never delves into erotica, let alone pornography, it also has a naughty side to it that is ever present and somewhat refreshing.

As Ried explains in his afterword, he grew up reading Tolkien but got fed up with the lack of sex in his work. "If I were a wizard and could cast real spells then would I not want to bedazzle some supermodels, magically acquire plenty of gold and create my own kingdom?" he asks.

And, really, that's exactly what he's done with the *Medford Family Chronicles*. Bring on book three!

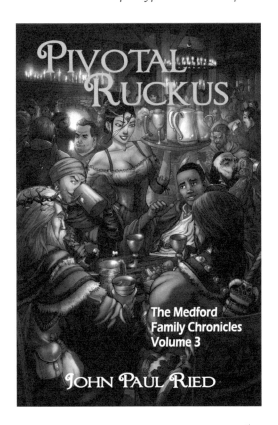

JOHN PAUL RIED

PIVOTAL RUCKUS

THE MEDFORD FAMILY CHRONICLES #3

PUBLISHER:
AZ PUBLISHING SERVICES

PUBLICATION DATE:
DECEMBER 2016

If *Reckless Ambitions*, the first volume in the ongoing *Medford Family Chronicles*, was a problem and its first sequel, *Capricious Deities*, was a solution, then *Pivotal Ruckus* is perhaps half of each.

Cut ruthlessly down to its core elements, *Reckless Ambitions* was a gigantic collection of archetypes and conveniences that served to introduce us to a world, an empire and the people who make it tick. Author John Paul Ried poured so much passion into it that it became infectious, even with an oversimplification on every third page, and a plot convenience and a crazy character motivation filling the pair in between. *Capricious Deities*, however, successfully avoided most of those problems, focusing instead on a single battle that worked on the macro scale of kingdoms colliding and the micro scale of the local folk who got dragged into it because it happened to unfold right on top of their town.

Rather annoyingly, *Pivotal Ruckus* does both of these things.

Like *Capricious Deities*, easily the best book in the series thus far, this is another focused story, this time taking place on and around the Forsaken Islands, four days north of Paladon City by ship. There are a pair of these. A mountain on the western island houses a 250' purple dragon called Kildarious Sharpclaw, who's been mysteriously quiet for a few generations, so it's the eastern island where the humans live. We meet a host of new characters there, who spend the early chapters living and loving and passing their time. Of course, this changes a little when Gargamel-eche, a nine-foot-tall flying gargoyle who's an ambassador for the Empire of Kasavemel, storms into the Screaming Ghost tavern to proclaim that this empire will be invading in four or five months time.

Now, while he and his cohorts are clearly outnumbered on that night, this promised battle is as one-sided as you can imagine. On the human side, Bayton Township counts about five hundred residents, mostly an array of farmers. On the humanoid side (and, oddly, both sides do use this term), the Emperor Shapireten X has an armada of ten thousand ships and one million warriors, all supported by demons and magicians. How this battle is going to be remotely believable is the biggest task Ried sets himself this time out and it has to be said that he has to cheat a little to make it work. However, the Forsaken Islanders do build up an army and navy and write up plans for all eventualities.

What Ried does best is to manage all this. It betrays his background in role playing games, because this is clearly the work of a dungeon-master translated into literature, rather than the work of a novelist. For the most part, he moves the right pieces around his virtual board, bulking up here and preparing there, readying his players for a fantastic night of gaming. This is the *Capricious Deities* half of the affair.

What he does worst is to convince us of the details of it all and that's the *Reckless Ambitions* half. There is a simplicity of assumption that applies throughout and which is also obviously sourced from the games that spawned this series. Wealth never runs out. Sex solves everything. Every accomplishment results in a promotion. Every question has an answer. Most of all, everyone picks up skills just like that. And, from a town of five hundred people, they adapt to scale impeccably! Hey, you need a palatial estate? Well, my farmer boyfriend has hammered two bits of wood together before. Cool, he can be my foreman!

In between those two, depending on your perspective, is where he's planning to go with the naughty angle. In my review of *Capricious Deities*, I highlighted that the inclusion of a sexual element, without ever venturing into erotica, was one of the strong points of the series. It's just as subject to that simplicity of assumption as anything else (So I have to be this enemy leader's concubine while obtaining intel, grandpa? OK, that's no problem), but it's a welcome addition to a genre that usually avoids it or goes overboard with it.

However, there are some more dubious angles exhibited here and some may find them objectionable. For example, the oldest profession apparently carries no stigma at all on the Forsaken Islands, so the best whore at the Screaming Ghost is the "belle of the town". Grace can even have a boyfriend, they can be madly in love and the townsfolk can place bets on when they'll be married. It's all fine. It's a little strange to see her jealous of any girl who even looks at Joseph, and he certainly can't look back while she screws anyone for cash. I don't buy that, but that's just credibility on the line.

The really objectionable angle is logical, in that, if whoredom is respectable, then girls can fairly see it as a career choice. Thus Emma Hutchinson, "a young, sixteen-year-old blossoming beauty", can be Grace's protégé at the Screaming Ghost, where she's eager to follow in her older friend's footsteps. The auction for her virginity is a lively affair, conducted in front of nobility after a seductive dance, and "her services for the evening" are promptly won by Captain Harvey Taylor, a 38-year-old ship's captain, who spends a ridiculous sum on her. What's perhaps most outrageous is that this is the start of a beautiful friendship that soon blossoms into romance and then ends in marriage. I really don't want to be that guy and suggest restrictions on what authors can write, but Ried could have handled this in a much safer manner.

There are other angles that seem rather ill-advised too. It's bad enough for Gargemeleche to talk like an illiterate Alabama slave, but adding a surname of Hottentot is just wrong. Ried's ideas for names tend to be good ones, but he goes rather off the deep end with some here, especially with non-human characters. I quite like Sergeant Belchero Drinkswill and even Admiral Battemhard, but naming an old troll commodore Sosueme Wedafuquawe? No. Don't even get me started on the god who's named, and I kid you not, Bidoodleoboop.

The other problem with names is that Ried seems to believe that we want to hear full names in every line of dialogue, even when they're not official proclamations. Nobody would ever say, "My wife Lady Cecilia Ann Menelynn Medford died in the same Scarlet Fever epidemic that same year," or "Ever since the civil war ended five months ago, our new Palamaran Emperor Thomas Wilson Oakley Medford IV has been obsessed with building all sorts of ships." They'd just say "my wife" or "our new emperor".

All in all, this sits very much in between the previous two books. While it remains just as much fun, it's a step down in quality from *Capricious Deities*, though not so far as *Reckless*

Ambitions. The fourth book in the series will be called *Academic Mayhem*, so presumably will return some focus to the Gamemasters University, which stepped back from this one. With it, I hope Ried can keep his worldbuilding skills and his recognisable sense of passion, while keeping his plot conveniences down and giving his characters plenty more believable motivations.

79

DAVID B. RILEY

FALLEN ANGEL

PUBLISHER:
HADROSAUR PUBLICATIONS
PUBLICATION DATE:
FEBRUARY 2019

Wow, was this a wild trip! It's a short novel, perhaps short enough to be a novella, that follows on from some other books by David B. Riley that I had completely failed to realise were related. At least I own copies of "The Two Devils", "The Devil's Due" and "The Dust Devil", so I can catch up with them in months to come. I'd think that reading them first will help but I was able to keep up starting here.

Anyone who's met Riley at a convention will immediately associate him with a genre that's known as weird west. He's written a number of novels and he also publishes an annual magazine, *Science Fiction Trails*. I've bought a few books from him but this is the first one I've sat down to read. And, boy, have I been missing out!

Our heroine, because I believe we can call her that, is Mabel Saunders, the fallen angel of the title, an epithet we should take literally. Yes, she is an actual angel, kicked out of Heaven and resident in Hell. However, she's very much an exception to all the rules you can imagine. God (who makes an interesting cameo here) has given her a key to the Kingdom of Heaven, which she wears round her neck, and Nick Mephistopheles seems to be pretty lax on the security front, letting Mabel wander around the Earth rather a lot.

We first meet her at Vicksburg in 1963, where Mabel's working as a nurse, alongside her cannibal nympho sister Kevin (yeah, I never expected to use those four words in that order either) and a couple of others. They're not just doing their bit for the soldiers working for General Grant (a personal friend of Mabel's), they're doing their bit to thwart an invasion of little green men from Mars, who show up in their shining balls of light and shoot at people with their ray guns.

The tone throughout is ever flippant and naughty (it's family-friendly language all the way through and there are no sex scenes, but, wow, does plenty get suggested!), enough so that it's not too surprising to find ourselves on a quick jump forward to the San Francisco of 1884.

Mabel's unchanged, just as much of a wish-fulfilment girl as ever. She's totally out of time for this era, being confident and sassy, able to drink beer and play cards with the men in sleazy saloons and even bum cigars off them as she does so. She kicks ass, of course, and she's rather free with her favours, too. She is held by some rules, but she holds herself by some others that confuse people, namely that she counterfeits money but refuses to cheat at cards.

Her beau, though I have to wonder how they met and how they stay together, given that she keeps flitting off to Hell and returning years later at the exact same age, is Special Agent Miles O'Malley of the U.S. Treasury. The answer to that puzzle will be in one of those prior books, I'm sure, which may or may not follow him rather than Mabel. Anyway, she tracks him down in Deadwood where he's following up on a lead that the Sioux have a Martian prisoner.

Needless to say, this is wild and wacky stuff. Riley plays it for laughs, whether with dry wit, surreal dialogue, recurring gags or wildly ludicrous situations. I'll surely never see the University of California at Berkeley the same way ever again, but I enjoyed Madam Veronica's dominatrix parlour, the constant to and fro of the devil's gun (which never misses) and even a lot of the Martian scenes, though they're more of a running gag than plot material here.

The writing is unpolished, in that it really needs a fresh proofreading job and some tidying up. The storytelling is done very much on the surface with the humour and surreality there to keep us going. That side is handled well because it's often gloriously funny, but the actual story (or stories) are undeveloped and almost an afterthought.

Perhaps there would seem to be more depth if I'd got to know the characters first in the prior volumes. I have a feeling that this is less of a sequel, though, and more of an opportunity to have fun with regular characters that we should know from those earlier books. Certainly, they look a great deal more substantial on my shelves.

This is a fun ride for 130 pages and I have to say that it makes me want to read more of Riley's work, but it's pretty flimsy stuff that deserved to be given more space to develop. This seems like Riley taking his characters and having fun with them, which is fine and highly enjoyable, but if he'd have spent more time fleshing out the story around them, this could have been a great 250-page novel.

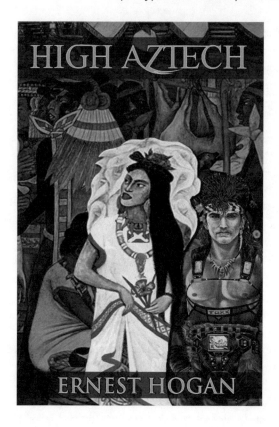

ERNEST HOGAN

HIGH AZTECH

PUBLISHER:
CREATESPACE

PUBLICATION DATE:
MAY 2016

Over the last couple of years, I've worked my way through all the books that Emily Devenport has published under her various pseudonyms and I've enjoyed how she clearly writes what she wants to write rather than what a publisher might happen to prefer. That apparently goes double for her husband, Ernest Hogan, as I have to say that I've never read anything quite like *High Aztech* before!

That said, it's not too tough to see the influences. This is paranoid gonzo cyberpunk, an amalgam of Hunter S. Thompson and Philip K. Dick, but phrased from a completely different ethnic background, which has led to Hogan being fairly described as "the father of Chicano science fiction". It could be seen as a sort of road movie, given that the lead charac-

ter doesn't actually do much except be passed from one captivity to another, serving as both an unwilling and unwitting guide to a rather mad future.

He's Xólotl Zapata and he begins this novel as a poet and comic book writer in the Mexico City of 2045, now known once more as Tenochtitlán because the world is wildly different from the one we live in today. Armageddon happened, as a nuclear war in the Middle East that practically wiped out monotheistic faith and left North America in ruins. Science and medicine come out of Africa now and Mexico is rising again as a polytheistic Aztec nation.

What's left of the US is now a racist Christian fundamentalist nation and, get this for a novel originally published in 1992, there's a southern border wall, a Tortilla Curtain, to keep the heathen pagan Aztecs out of God's own country. It's not complete because people keep on blowing it up, whether they're Aztec or "freedom-loving Americans". The government agents we meet see whoever it is as being in league with Satan. I mention all this for its prescience but it's hardly the focus of the book.

The focus seems to be Zapata trying to escape a succession of fates. At the start of the book, he's sentenced to death by the Neliyacme, a street gang who have taken offence at his usage of their leader as a template for one of his characters, but they have to wait in line to kill him because the story shoves ahead of them and everyone else suddenly wants him too. That's mostly because he's infected with a virus by his girlfriend, Cóatliquita, but not a traditional one.

This virus is a religion, which is a glorious concept. In particular, it's the Aztec religion which is making something of a comeback in Tenochtitlán, with televangelists calling for people to have their hearts removed in sacrifices to the gods but replaced by artificial equivalents so they can live on in their good graces. Starting there, humanoid tacos suddenly make utter sense.

Anyway, Zapata is no diehard follower of the Aztec ways until he's infected and now all he can do is look forward to a flowery death as a warrior, while touching everyone he can to infect them too. What's most wonderful here is that this doesn't work as an either/or. If the virus infects a person of no particular faith, then they gain it and powerfully too, but, if it infects a person who already has faith, then it combines with it to create a hybrid of the two. As you can imagine, that soon gets weird, and

Hogan is blissfully happy to make it as weird as he can. One late chapter is truly joyous.

Having been sentenced to death by someone, infected with Aztec religion by someone else and seduced by another someone, Zapata finds himself promptly bounced around a whole bunch more someone elses until we can figure out exactly what's going on and who's behind it all. There are a lot of wild groups, gangs and organisations in Tenochtitlán and they all apparently want Zapata for their own reasons: the evangelists, the mafia, the street gangs, foreign agents, the pepenadores who recycle the garbage, even Zapata's old friend, Itzcóatl O'Gorman and his Surrealist Terrorist Voodoo Network.

And Hogan tells all this, rather appropriately, in a rather bizarre hybrid language. He writes in English but his characters frequently dip into what's known as Españahuatl, an unholy merger of Mexican Spanish and Nahuatl, the native tongue of Mexico. This is instantly daunting but surprisingly easy to grasp. For all the myriad words we don't understand that Hogan dips his dialogue into, he deliberately keeps it understandable.

"Get the xixatl away from me, you ocotitotl maricóntl!" includes almost as many words I don't know as those I do, but the meaning is clear and we don't need to consult the glossary until we've finished the book, just to see how much we got right. I should add that Españahuatl isn't the easiest language to pronounce, but it's not the long words that are problematic, like the few mentioned above or the names of the many Aztec gods, or even the key word "ticmotraspasarhuililis"; it's words with far too many vowels right next to each other, like "jodioaing", that are the most overt reason why I'm never going to attempt to read this aloud to my wife.

There's a lot here to take in, because it's hurled at us at rapid speed and we keep on moving. Every time we come to terms with what one of these groups does and why, we're bounced on to another, like the ball in a game of ulama. Every one is there to serve as social comment and, not being Mexican, I can be pretty sure that I didn't grasp everything that Hogan wants to impart. I did get some of it though and it rings very true.

Perhaps that's why I like the characters more than I should. I found them a quirky bunch but I'm pretty sure they're archetypes, just not ones I tend to recognise. I like how they don't appear how they should, with a pair of characters spouting on racial issues while neither of them being of the race that they then resemble, courtesy of the plastic surgery masters in Guadalajara. That reminds that there's a heck of a lot of technology here, used like Philip K. Dick would as ways to shape the background. It is 2045 after all.

I adored this. It's not the most polished book I've ever read and it breaks most of the rules of fiction that I can name, but it's wild and weird and wonderful and I'm happy with that. It's also fiercely original, doing things that I've never seen done before between the pages of a book. I am annoyed with myself for taking so long to track this novel down and I'm now frantic to find *Cortez on Jupiter* and *Smoking Mirror Blues*. Hopefully they're equally as cuallioso.

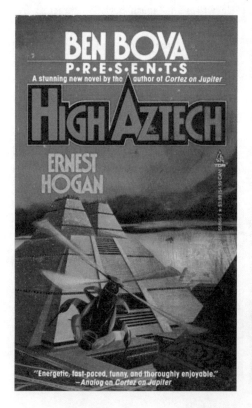

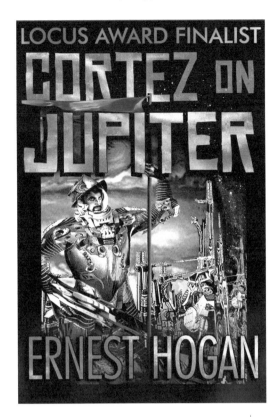

ERNEST HOGAN

CORTEZ ON JUPITER

PUBLISHER:
STRANGE PARTICLE PRESS
PUBLICATION DATE:
SEPTEMBER 2014

I'm having an absolutely blast this month with different cultural voices in the science fiction I'm reading. I explored a god-drenched Lagos in the Suyi Davies Okungbowa debut, *David Mogo, Godhunter* and I also booked a return trip to the unique mind of Ernest Hogan for his debut, *Cortez on Jupiter*. I adored *High Aztech*, as ruthlessly unusual as it was, and yearned for more.

Now I've read this, I think I can safely say that I preferred Hogan's follow-up to this, but that's entirely appropriate for first and second novels. We should always get better. However, I thoroughly enjoyed this too and some of these scenes and ideas are surely going to stay with me. What's more, the sheer audacity of what Hogan attempted here deserves its own

praise because this is truly imaginative, something that we should be able to say about every sf novel but usually can't.

We're here to find out why Pablo Cortez is a celebrity. He must be one because the book is built like a documentary on him, interspersing interview clips with him in his zero gravity splatterpaint studio and those of other people filling in gaps in his story from their own perspectives. But why is he a celebrity? If you take that not as a simple question but as the theme to a novel, *Cortez on Jupiter* will make a lot more sense and seem a little less weird.

Ben Bova picked this up for his *Discoveries* series of paperbacks and published it in 1990. That means that it predates what we understand as reality TV and a lot of the soundbiteinfused American docu-drama style that television pitches to sufferers of ADD today. Yet Hogan nailed it. I see the Odysseus mission to Jupiter as a much more biting a jab at reality TV than *Rollerball* and *The Running Man* or other famous takes on future media. And yet that doesn't seem to be the point, except that it is. The most telling line in the book is when Pablo Cortez invents splatterpainting on a zero gravity flight and his friend is devastated because he didn't record it.

Cortez starts out as a nobody who thinks he's a somebody. He's a Chicano graffito in Los Angeles and he can't stand being part of the mainstream. He's punk and outsider and ruthlessly driven by his own sense of integrity and, let's admit it, his rampaging ego. He hijacks a set of art students and turns them into a bona

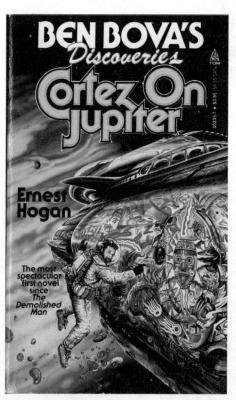

fide movement, the Guerrilla Muralists of Los Angeles. They mount a set of publicity stunts in the holy name of art, things like detonating paint bombs so that an entire three mile area around the Civic Center turns orange.

When they're stopped, because of course they're stopped, most of them start to behave again because they're law abiding citizens and that's how they've been conditioned. Pablo, on the other hand, uses the notoriety he gained to move on up, literally. He wangles his way onto the Space Culture Project, frustratedly trying to give them what they want so that he can do what he wants, but never manages it satisfactorily because the idea of doing what someone else wants simply isn't who he is. Everything is about him and his art, pure and unfettered.

He has to do things that haven't been done before and that's what leads him to Jupiter, because you know from the title that he was going to get there. There are microorganisms inside the Great Red Spot and they're intelligent, though in a way that we've never before encountered. We certainly can't communicate with them, so the Odysseus Project is lowering people into the Great Red Spot to try to find out how to do that. And they're consistently dying. Somehow, and this really doesn't count as a spoiler because a) it's detailed on the back cover blurb and b) it's brought up early in the novel as the start of the great Pablo Cortez documentary, he's the one who manages to do so, channelling the Sirens of Jupiter into a new and vibrant form of art.

This is wildly imaginative stuff but it's also told through wildly imaginative language. This novel is often seen as the creation of Chicano SF because Hogan wrote it with a Chicano voice. It's more in English than *High*

Aztech but it's really told in a sort of Spanglish, the foundation of English enhanced with an abundance of Spanish words whenever applicable. And it isn't just the inclusion of Spanish that makes it so wild. There are names as utterly glorious as Nuke Damballah and the following line isn't remotely unusual:

> "Hey, maybe there was something about ATL causing mutations, or maybe it's because I was raised neo-Aztec in a relocated barrioid then ended up in a paleofuturoid instant suburb fighting a psychwar with the melting pot upwardly mobile SoCal zombies."

Yeah, it's that sort of novel. But it's also a celebration of ego, the artist's confidence that he's right and everyone else is wrong. It's a look at what art really is, because the book is phrased as a work of art, albeit a written take on an audiovisual piece rather than a splatterpainting. It's about integrity. It's about exploitation. It's about dedication.

And it's inherently, fundamentally, totally about sacrifice. It's about how a true artist is a starving artist, because a starving artist is an honest artist and he chooses to sacrifice convenience and easy commerciality for his own very personal vision of value and truth. It's also clearly about literal sacrifice because I haven't read all the Aztec symbology in Hogan's novels to not read the dipping of live volunteers into the Great Red Spot of Jupiter, knowing that they'll surely die on camera, as a form of ritual human sacrifice, especially as nobody feels that bad about dead Sirenauts if the viewers are still tuning in.

There's a lot here, though a great deal of it isn't traditional science fiction in the slightest. And, it must be said, that's a major reason why I love Hogan's unashamedly gonzo take on the genre so deeply.

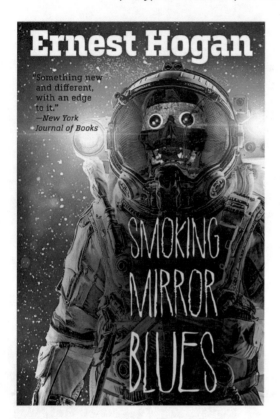

ERNEST HOGAN

SMOKING MIRROR BLUES

PUBLISHER:
STRANGE PARTICLE PRESS

PUBLICATION DATE:
APRIL 2018

There's such an amazing and varied pool of talent in this state that it somehow feels unfair to return to an author I've read before for my Arizona book this month, but Ernest Hogan wrote three novels and I've only read and reviewed two. This catches me up.

Hogan's writing is more joyously unlike that of anyone else out there than any other local author I've had the privilege to read thus far, even his wife, Emily Devenport, who also emphatically writes very much on her own terms. That's because he writes gonzo even more than he writes science fiction and he does it with such a unique style. He may start this book by describing the costume of Phoebe Graziano as "some kind of neomythical recombocultural chimera" but I think he's really describing himself.

He isn't a prolific novelist. *Cortez on Jupiter* and *High Aztech* came out in the early nineties, while the genesis of this one goes even further back, but it finally saw the light of day in 2001 and could be seen as wrapping up a thematic trilogy. These books are gonzo glimpses of futuristic Chicano culture through a science fictional lens, all wrapped up in Aztec mythology and the creative process, with definition of deity central to all three of them.

To aid their unique flavour, they're told in a new language that's part English, part Spanish and part Nahuatl, along with a few words that I'm sure Hogan invented entirely out of new cloth. Turn this to any random page and you'll probably find someone describing something as either "sumato" or "xau-xau". Neither word is Googleable but their meanings are relatively clear, if occasionally muddled a little by an ever-evolving mindset. It's as if Hogan serves as a recurring window on a future world but each glimpse is just a little off in time from the last and slang has moved on without us.

This consistency but fluidity is fascinating to me. Reading Hogan is kind of like getting drawn against our will into the channel the Burger King in Gila Bend is always playing—I think it's TMZ—and trying without any grounding in teen culture to figure out what reality it's selling. I have no idea who these celebrities are and I don't understand their cultural references or language. It's like individual words are familiar but not in the order they're given. I don't know what it is, but it's likely sumato and it may well be xau-xau.

The central idea of *Smoking Mirror Blues* is that Beto Orozco, who's a game designer in Los Angeles, finds himself possessed by Tezcatlipoca, the trickster god of the Aztecs, after conjuring him up as an AI and unwisely going into a trance at precisely the wrong moment. This coincides with a festival called Dead Daze, an American bastardisation of the Mexican Days of the Dead, and that gives Tezcatlipoca the opportunity to wreak all sorts of havoc on the city of Angels.

In many ways, this is a supernatural battle of a novel. Tezcatlipoca, newly reborn and neatly connected to Beto's knowledge and the internet mediasphere, starts to seize power. He's aided by the corporate sponsored gang known as Los Olvidadoids—I recognise that from Luis Buñuel's movie *Los Olvidados*, or *The Young and the Damned*—and a street band who go by Los Tricksters. Beto continues to struggle to resurface inside his own body and a number of wildly varied players in this game come together to do battle with the resurrected deity.

They're so varied and so fun that I'd almost love to see who would be cast in their roles in some indie film version with budget. I say "almost" because nobody could do these books justice and I'm not sure I really want to see anyone try. We'd really need a Hispanic version of Lance Mungia, who directed *Six-String Samurai*, or maybe Jim Jarmusch, if he spent his entire time on the project high on speed. This couldn't play slowly; it's a colourful riot that would need to explode onto the screen to challenge an ADHD audience and win.

Some parts have natural choices to fill them. I could totally see Bai Ling as Madam Tan Tien, but I've no idea who would play her seven-foot-tall partner in both tantric sex

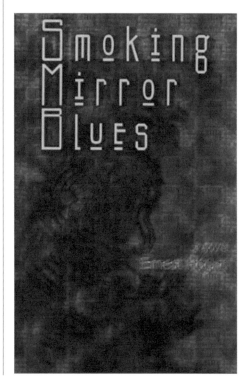

practices and Ti-Yong/Hoodoo Investigations, Zobop Delvaux. Who would fill the ample boots of Caldonia, an African American force of nature with whom Phoebe sleeps when she's not with Beto or Smokey Espejo, the sumato persona that Tezcatlipoca adopts? It may be easier to cast the creator of the god simulation program, Xochitl Echaurren, and her robot guard dog, Santo.

Just to keep us on our toes, Hogan doesn't alternate chapters between different characters the way a majority of authors would with this story; he alternates pages, even paragraphs sometimes, as if we're absorbing this story from the Bloomberg channel. There's a television crew documenting Dead Daze, who become our Greek chorus. There's also a wildcard organisation of religious fanatics called Earth Angels, who promise to get in everyone's way and complicate everything.

While "traditional" is the last word I really want to use to describe anything with Hogan's name on it, I think this plays a little more traditionally than his other two novels, at least when it comes down to the core story. It's still out there structurally otherwise. And I don't think I learned as much as I did in *High Aztech*, which has the side effect of making this easier to read aloud when yo no hablo Español, let alone Nahuatl. Tezcatlipoca is just cake compared to names like Huitzilopochtli and Tenyotecuhtli, let alone a catchphrase as wild as "ticmotraspasarhuililis", an important word in *High Aztech*.

What I did learn is what the title means. *Smoking Mirror* is a direct English translation of a Nahuatl name, that of the central character, Tezcatlipoca. It speaks to Mesoamerican mirrors that were made of obsidian and used in shamanic rituals. Suddenly, the psychedelic

Texan trio, Smokey Mirror, who blew me away on stage before COVID locked us down, are even more sumato than I thought they were. That reference had whizzed right past me at the time. Chingow!

Now, where can I download me some Los Tricksters and which episodes of *Lucha Underground* did they introduce musically?

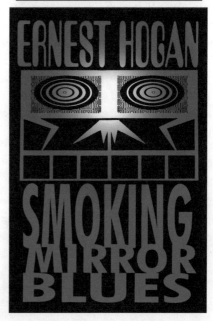

SUYI DAVIES OKUNGBOWA

DAVID MOGO, GODHUNTER

PUBLISHER:
ABADDON BOOKS
PUBLICATION DATE:
JULY 2019

I prefer my urban fantasy when it does something different, often by situating its story somewhere unusual. I was fortunate enough to be on a signing session with Suyi Davies Okungbowa at TusCon in 2019 and I couldn't resist his pitch. I promptly picked up a copy of this, which I believe is his debut novel, because it didn't sound remotely like anything I've read before and that's exactly what I found when actually reading it.

They do say that authors should write what they know and Okungbowa knows Lagos, the former capital of Nigeria, because he was born there and, when he's not in Tucson, Arizona working on his MFA, he continues to live there. It naturally become the setting for this novel, in which he visits a fascinating calamity upon it. Put simply, the gods have fallen and they've taken over Lagos Island, or Èkó Ìsàlẹ̀, and it probably won't taken long before they start to expand.

While I believe Okungbowa trawls in gods from more than one pantheon, the vast majority here are Yoruba deities, or orishas, a mostly new mythology to me and a deep one. We gradually discover that the fiery gods, Aganju and Sango, have mounted a failed revolt in Orun, the traditional home of the orishas, and the result is that Obatala kicked a whole bunch of them out and effectively locked the gate behind them. Now Lagosians aren't just worried about when their power might go out today, but also what the gods are getting up to in their city.

Enter our protagonist, David Mogo, who's an orisha 'daji or demigod. He doesn't remember his parents, because he was brought up by a wizard, Papa Udi, but he does see his mother in visions. She's certainly an orishi, even if he doesn't know which one. That, like most things here, comes clear over time and we just need to be patient. For now, it's about David and what he's hired to do.

Lukmon Ajala, who's a local Baálè or clan head, as well as what the back cover blurb enticingly and accurately calls a "wizard gangster", wants him to locate and deliver Ibeji, twin orisha of vitality, to him. David takes the job for no better reason than he can't afford to replace his roof and he's half done in a shake of a lamb's tail, successfully delivering Taiwo, one of the twins. While the back cover blurb goes no further, however, it doesn't take long for that plot to change, and, talking with Kehinde, the other twin, he realises why he has to change it.

I won't go any further than that, because this is less like a novel and more a set of three linked novellas, this being the setup for the first. Knowing what the second one is spoils the first and so on. Instead, I'll suggest that it all reads a lot closer to Max Gladstone's deity-infused cities, like Dresidiel Rex in *Two Serpents Rise*, with its Aztec mythology and gods, than anything I've read by Nigerian authors like Nnedi Okorafor. Lagos merely happens to also be real.

It also feels far more immersive than Okorafor's *Binti* books for a number of reasons. While they saw Nigeria as a starting point, they moved far beyond it. Okungbowa never takes us out of Lagos, though we do explore a lot of it, visiting its major landmarks, like the Third Mainland Bridge, as well as rougher areas that locals wouldn't tell tourists about. We also feel the city because, for much of the book, it's shorn of its residents. Its streets are empty here, even if danger is secreted in their shadows.

The story also has its roots far deeper into Yoruba culture than *Binti* ever did in Igbo culture, partly again because we never leave Lagos but also partly because we care about a lot more local characters; there are no aliens here to distract us. I liked how Okungbowa explained the culture within its own bounds but often didn't translate it into something recognisable to a wider audience. He hints, that "Danfos" and "kekes" are transportation but not what sort, and we can understand if not remotely visualise "aso-ebi uniforms", "gele headpieces" and "flowing agbadas". This immersion is good for us and for stories too.

And, most obviously, Okungbowa flavours his story with language. He wrote it in English but it's Nigerian English, which is very similar to but not quite the Queen's English. As an Englishman living in the States, I found it interesting to note that there are different differences, but they're no more jarring to the non-native reader. Papa Udi, however, speaks in pidgin English, which is much harder to follow, though far from impossible. I enjoyed figuring that out as I went.

What I couldn't figure out while reading and am happily looking up afterwards, is the use of accents on words, though this didn't spoil my enjoyment of the book. The Yoruba language is tonal and it utilises accents both above and below letters, and sometimes both, as in Èkó Ìsàlè. That may look weird on this screen, as an attempt to add such accents to Unicode was rejected. It comes up often too, as every vowel carries an accent, marking low, mid or high tone, and so does some uses of ṣ denoting a "sh" sound. I loved this immersion in language, even if I still struggle to pronounce any of these Yoruba words.

I loved the first novella of the three too, which is *Godhunter* and covers the search for Ibeji and the fallout from what that hunt sparks. It's exactly what this book needed to kick things off, introducing us to characters, both human and divine, the city itself and a whole slew of concepts and cultural details that we need to know for later. The second, *Firebringer*, is pretty good as well, an internal story for David Mogo to go with the external one he deals with in the first novella, which is a natural progression. Just as this is a story of Lagos, it's a story of David Mogo, who has just as much change to experience.

I had a little more trouble with the third, *Warmonger*, not because it's bad but because the story, by this point, started to seem somewhat inevitable. That may partly be because Okungbowa, for all that he clearly doesn't want to paint his story as good guys versus bad guys, only gives us an opportunity to see one of the two sides. Whenever we see the other, it's during a battle and, having got to that point with David Mogo, Papa Udi and their growing entourage, we're always going to see them as the heroes and the other guys as the villains.

Another reason is that those other characters do a lot more early in the book than they do late on when everything turns into the literary equivalent of a blockbuster's CGI boss battle. Remember *Wonder Woman* being fantastic for an hour and a half, but boring when it turned into a video game at the end? This isn't that bad in flow but there are surely similarities.

I liked a lot of the supporting characters here, such as Fati, a child bride rescued from Lukmon Ajala; Femi and the heroes of LASPAC, the Lagos State Paranormal Commission; and Shonuga and her horse at the Arena; but the endgame here was always going to be god vs. god and Okungbawa clearly can't see a viable place for any of these characters there, so they get inevitably sidelined, even if they do show up for something far above their mythological paygrade.

While this started better than it ended, I enjoyed it a great deal. As I hoped it would be, it's something completely different to anything I've read before. I look forward to seeing what Okungbawa comes up with next.

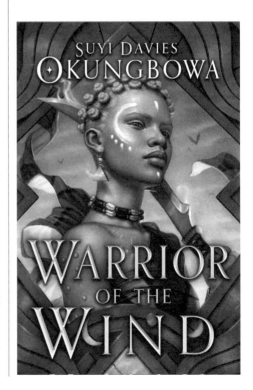

JOSEPH NASSISE

EYES TO SEE

JEREMIAH HUNT #1

PUBLISHER:
HARBINGER BOOKS
PUBLICATION DATE:
OCTOBER 2018

I've had *Watcher of the Dark*, the third of the *Jeremiah Hunt* trilogy, on my TBR shelf for quite a few years now and I've finally bitten the bullet and found the first two. I've read one other original novel by Nassise, *By the Blood of Heroes*, which was the opening volume of his *Great Undead War* series, and enjoyed it, so I was happy to find that this also mixes up genres.

Jeremiah Hunt feels like a private investigator, even though he isn't really one at all. He feels lived in, aware, driven. The trenchcoat and hat hardly hurt either. He's really a professional fish out of water, the most unusual ghost hunter I've yet met in fiction, partly because everything he does for money is subservient to his primary job of looking for his lost daughter.

This book is told through a set of chapters labelled THEN and even more NOW.

The THEN chapters read like a thriller, all told in italics. Hunt was a mild mannered translator of ancient documents working from home when Elizabeth, his young daughter, mysteriously vanishes from the house. He struggles not only with his loss but guilt at not keeping her safe while his wife was away. He dedicates his life to the search, so much so that his wife leaves him, but a darker time lies ahead.

In between the THEN and NOW chapters, we learn that he went further than the average guilt-ridden loving father of a lost daughter would go. He performed an ancient ritual that stole his sight from him in exchange for the ability to see beyond. What that translates to is no sight in daylight, better sight than the rest of us in pure darkness and the additional bonus of seeing the dead. All of them. And there are a heck of a lot of them around us.

The NOW chapters continue his quest to find Elizabeth, but they begin with a job, to force a powerful ghost victim to vanish from a building to allow its occupants, as undeserving as they are, to live in peace. It's there as a means to establish Hunt's talents but then he consults with the police on a murder and his professional life starts to interact with his personal one. What we're in on and he hasn't figured out yet is that someone wants him involved for reasons of their own, someone or something not human.

While the THEN chapters clearly read like a relatively traditional thriller, the NOW chapters are much harder to categorise. Certainly they don't continue in the thriller style, but can we call them urban fantasy? Maybe urban fantasy told through the filters of horror novel and hardboiled detective tale. Would it count as grimdark, given that it's fantastic but also acutely down and dirty? It might well. Even as a mixed genre piece, I think it would still play well to fans of straight horror.

Hunt is an interesting character a lot more than he's a likeable one. We do have sympathy for his situation as a parent who's lost a child but can't yet grieve for them, who has given frankly more than we probably would to locate her, who is still consumed by guilt for allowing it to happen on his watch. But that doesn't mean that we like him because he's not particular likeable, so dedicated is he to that one dominant task. We might admire his dedication while sneering at his wife for giving up so quickly, but we do understand a lot of why she left.

He dominates here almost completely, even though there are other characters with whom he works or from whom he seeks help. The former means a Boston homicide detective called Miles Stanton, while the latter comprise Denise Clearwater, who's a witch, and Dmitri Alexandrov, a mysterious Russian who runs an Irish pub in Dorchester. To be fair, they all justify their respective page counts but don't come close to stealing any of our attention from Hunt.

The only characters that appeal to us as much as Hunt are the two ghosts who help him out the most, Whisper and Scream. The latter is a hulking presence with the ability to instill dread so intense that he's a powerful repellent, while the former is a little girl who allows him to see through her eyes, an

important thing because ghostsight is not like regular sight at all and that is a huge deal to Hunt. Neither can speak and we don't have any identity or background, but both clearly have stories for us to eventually learn.

It's interesting to discover, after we finish the novel, that Nassise had an entirely different ending for this book planned originally and that's in my Harbinger trade paperback edition as a bonus. I won't explain what's in the old ending or the new ending or detail why they're fundamentally different, but I will say that I'm rather happy at this juncture that his publisher in Germany, where this first volume initially saw print, talked him into a different way forward entirely. It certainly doesn't stop me wanting to continue right on into *King of the Dead*, but I'll reevaluate that ending afresh at the point I finish that one.

I'm also tempted to drop a hint because I snipped my synopsis in the bud at a pretty early point in the novel. It takes a long while to get to where we understand what's going on and it isn't a mystery we're going to solve from information dropped within the book; we pretty much have to wait for Hunt to figure it out and pass that back to us. So I'll add that this unfolds in New England, Boston to be precise, and that location proves notably important. I don't think that spoils anything and it won't mean anything until you're at the point where things are revealed, but it allows me to point out that I'm appreciative of the depth of background that we end up with.

JOSEPH NASSISE

KING OF THE DEAD

JEREMIAH HUNT #2

PUBLISHER:
HARBINGER BOOKS

PUBLICATION DATE:
NOVEMBER 2018

The title *King of the Dead* seems to be reserved for sequels. It's *Lens of the World #2, The Lost Slayer #3* and *Ravenloft #15*, but here it's the second in the *Jeremiah Hunt* trilogy, in between *Eyes to See* and *Watcher of the Dark*. My Harbinger trade paperback edition, however, may be the only *King of the Dead* to feature a "click here" image in print. Ugh.

Problems with the Harbinger edition aside, I enjoyed this novel a lot. It's a progression from the first, of course, but less focused on Jeremiah Hunt, now that he's part of a team, and more traditional in its approach to story. *Eyes to See* is all about Hunt, even if there are other characters in there to help or hinder his quest for his daughter, and his grief at losing her in bizarre circumstances is so palpable that it's almost his unwanted sidekick. That's taken care of before this book begins, so the tone is different.

Also, *Eyes to See* alternated between thriller and urban fantasy, with more than a little borrowed from the horror and hardboiled detective genres. This is urban fantasy through and through, though the horror aspects do continue to be obvious. Hey, this is about a king of the dead and the cover art on the various editions isn't misleading.

A quick recap: Hunt is a translator of ancient manuscripts whose daughter was abducted from his house while he was working. His emotional devastation, as well as his single-minded dedication to finding her, destroyed his marriage and led to him performing a ritual that left him blind in daylight but able to see beyond our realm. He sees and interacts with ghosts, who lend him what he calls ghostsight, something useful in book one but fundamental in book two.

Crucially, while Hunt and his companions

do find resolution to everything that's thrown at them in *Eyes to See*, they do so in ways that the regular world can't accept. In other words, while Hunt is one of the good guys, the FBI, who were investigating the same string of murders he was, know beyond a shadow of a doubt that he's the Reaper. They have a video in which he kills someone on camera! Of course it's him! They can't know that it was really a doppelganger of an ancient sorcerer who's now been defeated. To them, Hunt is a wanted man in an active case and so he's on the run.

Where to go, other than out of Boston, is an open question that's answered by one of his cohorts, a witch called Denise Clearwater. She is experiencing visions that tell her that there's trouble in New Orleans and she needs to go there to help stop it. And so they hit the road, Hunt and Clearwater and Dmitri Alexandrov, who turns into a polar bear when needs must. Eventually, of course, they face off against the King of the Dead.

It takes a while to get to that point though. Joseph Nassise builds this in a steady manner, establishing a new dynamic for this novel with a team made up of three Gifted, two of whom are technically on the run. When they get to New Orleans, he lets us in on some of the infrastructure of the supernatural world in this universe, the local Lord Marshal doing everything he can in a trying situation when everyone on the Council is dead and gone. It helps us feel more grounded and I'm sure Hunt feels that too.

What's happening stays unexplained until Hunt's able to lend his own particular talents to the search. People are dying of an unknown disease. They go into a sort of coma and then they die. It's a hundred percent fatal and, even if the regular doctors don't know this, every victim is Gifted. In fact, that's why every member of the Council in New Orleans is dead. This disease doesn't care how powerful someone is. It just kills them.

It's Hunt who figures out that it really isn't a disease at all. His talent allows him to see auras or souls and he realises right off the bat that none of the victims have one any more, even if they haven't died yet. That means that someone or something is taking those souls and, without venturing into what I'd see as spoiler territory, Hunt figures that out too, with that knowledge serving as the breakthrough that what's left of the Gifted community in New Orleans needs to move forward.

While the structure is pretty straightforward for urban fantasy and we know from the very title of the book that there's going to be a king of the dead behind everything, Nassise is a writer who can milk this by adding a worthy amount of texture and impact. We aren't just watching this all happen from a remove, we're in the thick of it with Hunt and Clearwater and her old coven mate, Simon Gallagher, who's Lord Marshal long before his time. While we're rarely surprised by what happens, we react well when it does.

And all of this makes this trilogy seem like it shouldn't be a trilogy. The first book played like a feature, telling its own story and wrapping it up neatly at the end. It could easily have been a standalone novel. Nassise had meant for it to be a trilogy all along, but with Hunt continuing the search for his daughter throughout, something that his initial publisher baulked at and prompted him to change. And so it became a different trilogy.

This doesn't feel like the middle book in a trilogy at all. It feels like a second book in an open-ended series, like the opening episode in a TV series based on a feature. It takes all the setup that Nassise did in *Eyes to See* and translates it into a formula. Here are the stars, here's the structure, here are the dynamics by which it's all going to work. Now, rinse and repeat for another twenty-one episodes, with the series arc being the FBI searching for Hunt because they think he's the Reaper.

That makes me all the more intrigued by what *Watcher of the Dark* is going to end up being. If it was just episode two, it would be just like this but in a different city with different monsters to fight. But it's not; it's the final book in a trilogy. I'm looking forward to finding out what it's going to be like.

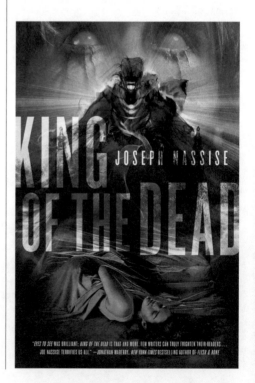

98

JOSEPH NASSISE

WATCHER OF THE DARK

JEREMIAH HUNT #3

PUBLISHER:
TOR

PUBLICATION DATE:
NOVEMBER 2013

This has been an odd month for wrapping up trilogies. The three Aubry Knight books by Steven Barnes were very different from each other but somehow still worked as a solid story arc for the lead and a trilogy. I'm not sure, however, that I can say that about the three Jeremiah Hunt books, because this doesn't feel a lot like a trilogy at all.

The first, *Eyes to See*, originally published in German, certainly aimed to begin a story arc that would run for three novels but that changed when that publisher persuaded him to shift a key element into the finalé of the opening volume. With his story arc stolen, he continued with the trilogy anyway but I feel that the second book, *King of the Dead*, changed things up, introducing a different tone, an ongoing grounding and a new story for what was clearly a core set of characters.

This third and final book feels like another *King of the Dead*, a new story in a new city and a good one too, but it's an episode in a series that's open-ended rather than the way it all wraps up. Nassise has written longer series, but, thus far, he's resisted going back to this one that's worthy of quite a lot more entries. I certainly want to keep on going into books four and five, but they don't exist in this universe.

Another oddity for this series, however long it might eventually run, is that each book seems like it would work well as a standalone. Certain things would be clearer if you read in order, but I think that someone could pick up *Watcher of the Dark*, knowing nothing about Jeremiah Hunt or his world, and enjoy it just as much as someone who's been reading avidly along all the way.

Hunt is an interesting urban fantasy lead. His back story is told in book one and I don't need to recap it here. Suffice it to say that a deal with a devil left him in a rather strange situation. The deal steals his sight, so that he can't see anything at all in daylight, but gives him the ability to see on another level. In darkness, he can see ghosts and other things around us at all times but invisible to us, and he can even borrow their ghostsight to see as they do, which is a little differently to us.

This all happened in Boston but, because he's now sought by the FBI for an apparently clear-cut murder, action shifts in book two to New Orleans. Hunt is on the road again this time, arriving in Los Angeles and promptly falling foul of the local Magister, who is a very different character to Simon in the last book,

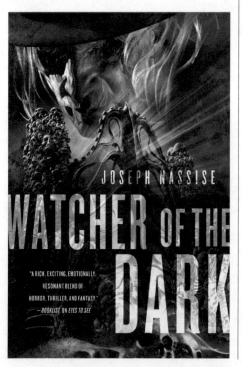

the Lord Marshall in New Orleans. It seems that the magical people in charge of cities don't have to worry about things checking their power and can be as good or bad as they want. Carlos Fuentes is definitely Gandalf as a mafia don, as Nassise puts it.

And he has an agenda. Outwardly upset that Hunt would waltz into his city and not let him know, he's really after Hunt's skills for a heist he's working, a heist that's a little different for a number of reasons. He's searching for a key, that's been broken into three pieces, each of which is kept hidden in a mysterious location. I wouldn't spoil what the key does except that the cover blurb does exactly that, so it's no mystery going in that it's a literal key to one of the gates of Hell.

While Hunt can't resist going along with Fuentes and his band of supernatural characters because he doesn't exactly have a heck of a lot of choice, it's a gimme that he really shouldn't let a corrupt Magister actually open the doors to Hell. The man already has one demon working for him. What a man like him could do with a whole army of them doesn't bear thinking about.

Clearly he must be stopped, but how can Hunt possibly achieve that? Not only is he blind during daylight, he's on his own. Denise Clearwater, the witch he worked with in the first two books, is still in the hospital after he stabbed her in the heart during the prior book (in order to save her life, I should add, as odd as that might sound). Their other companion, Dmitri Alexandrov, who happens to be a were-polar bear, is with her, so Hunt is on his own.

And there's a further catch, which again I wouldn't spoil except that Tor did just that on the dustjacket so it'll hardly be a surprise to readers of the hardback edition. A mysterious character called Preacher has floated through the series with his own mysterious agenda. He's the devil that Hunt dealt with to get his changed sight. He showed up again in *King of the Dead*, doing a favour for Hunt with the promise that he'd get one in return when he needed. Well, he calls in his marker in this book and that complicates things even more.

I've liked each of the previous Jeremiah Hunt books but I think the series is finding its feet at this point. Looking back, the first volume worked well as an origin story. It introduces Hunt and explains why he's the way he is, with some exploration of what he can and can't do. It also introduces a couple of companions and sets the stage. It's a great pilot before a TV show's opening season. *King of the Dead* was fun too, telling a self-contained story while expanding the world that Hunt lives in. This continues that with a new self-contained story and I think it's the best book of the three.

Hunt is developing as a human being here, but other characters are introduced who have as much quirky potential. Ilyana, the demon working for Fuentes, is a wild creature indeed, beautiful but scary, not least because she app-arently really enjoys eating spectres. Perkins is a human dowsing rod. Glenn Wagner, a victim of Fuentes's search, is a fascinating character far beyond that. The supernatural creatures they encounter expand the bestiary of Hunt's world as well.

And where they go and what they do is so much fun. One part of the key is in the base-ment of a Roman Catholic cathedral, which prompts a fantastic heist. I'd happily be on board for a series in which supernatural crea-tures don't go any further than breaking into cathedrals and stealing esoteric artifacts. A

broader story is just a bonus at that point!

Frankly, there are only two problems with this book. One is that it ends not just its own story but the Jeremiah Hunt series as a whole. I wanted this to carry on going for a while. How long do American TV show seasons run nowadays? Twenty-two episodes, right? I'd certainly tune in for the next nineteen! The other is that it ends a little too quickly. There's a lot of agreeable build, but when we get to the finalé, it ends sooner than it should.

Without any further Jeremiah Hunt novels to devour, there are at least plenty more Joseph Nassise novels. I've only read one thus far, the first in a series called *The Great Undead War*, an alternate history zombie novel by the name of *By the Blood of Heroes*, featuring an undead Red Baron. I had a blast with that too, so this trilogy has cemented Nassise as an author that I should seek out a lot more often.

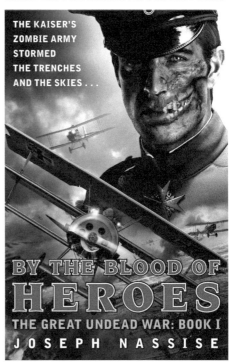

THE KAISER'S ZOMBIE ARMY STORMED THE TRENCHES AND THE SKIES...

BY THE BLOOD OF HEROES

THE GREAT UNDEAD WAR: BOOK I

JOSEPH NASSISE

S. C. MENDES

THE CITY

THE CITY SAGA #1

PUBLISHER:
BLOOD BOUND BOOKS

PUBLICATION DATE:
JANUARY 2019

OK, let's get this out of the way. S. C. Mendes is a pseudonym, I know who's behind it and I'm not going to tell you. I will, however, point out that he's a friend and I swapped his debut novel for one of mine. Now, it's always a dubious proposition to review books written by friends and acquaintances, because not all of them are great and some of them are pretty awful. I'm always an honest critic and I'd very much rather not review a book than slate it.

After reading the first couple of chapters of this one, I knew it wasn't one of those books by friends that suck. There was an odd phrase here and there that I thought could have ben-efitted from closer editing and the author was clearly more interested in characters than descriptions, but it wasn't a bad start at all, especially given where and when we start.

The City is set in San Francisco in 1910, so this is a period piece, even though it's not particularly interested in highlighting that. We don't feel we're walking under gaslamp-lit streets and we don't have much of a sense for the fashion or technology of the era. But we're also in Chinatown, which adds a lot of flavour, starting out in an opium den and soon finding our way to the brothel of Shin Sho, and I'm a sucker for anything period touching on the dark side of the Orient. Opium dens and puzzle boxes? I'm in.

Last night, I thought I'd read a few more chapters, but the damn thing took a firm hold of my throat and refused to let me go until I'd flipped the final page. It turns out that, while we technically remain around the San Francisco area throughout, we spend most of our time underneath the city, in the other city of the title, and that's a special place indeed, one that I'm going to have to be very careful not to spoil.

The back cover blurb doesn't actually take us far into the novel. Max Elliott was a police detective but, if he ever still thinks of himself as one, it's only because they put him on leave six months earlier rather than let him go. His wife, Eve, was murdered, in grisly fashion. Her bones were taken, leaving her carefully flensed skin and organs behind in a pile. Their

daughter, Leigh Anne, is still missing, but Max hasn't investigated much. He just took up an opium pipe and inhaled the guilt. He certainly didn't dedicate his life to an apparently fruitless quest, as Jeremiah Hunt did in *Eyes to See*.

Now, he had plenty of reason to feel guilty. He wasn't home when the unknown assailant killed his wife and took his daughter, because he was sleeping with Yanmei at the time in Shin Sho's brothel. Leigh Anne was twelve, Yanmei only eighteen. But he finally decides to do something about it, because his former partner, now Lt. Harris, wants him to investigate a new murder scene from the same killer. This time there are a trio of girls left without bones, chained up in the house of a dead man. Sure, he has a personal connection to the case, but Harris knows he's the best man to delve into something so dark.

The problem is that delving quickly takes him far beyond the jurisdiction of San Francisco's finest. Shin Sho identifies the drug left at the scene as si fen, made only by the Mara, about whom he refuses to say anything else. It's only when Max goes back to his old informant, Charlie Willis, that he finds a lead on the Mara, but it's a weird one. There's a way, through the Edge, with the right introduction and the right branding on your palm and... even though I'm only fifty some pages in, I'm going to stop right there. You need to buy a Shadow.

Frankly, if you dig original horror, you should read this book and you should experience the City without any preconceptions given to you by critics like me who don't shut up quickly enough. Let me just say that the author may not build much in the way of geography or detail, but he drenches the City in all the appropriate textures and tones for us to understand what it is and how it works. He also builds quite the culture, with its dumplings and skin puppets, colour-coded shows and progressively more brutal and decadent entertainments.

I can see where some of this came from, being an exploitation film fan. I've seen *Dumplings* and *Cannibal Holocaust*, not to forget *The Deer Hunter*, so I recognise snippets here and there, but this isn't a ripoff of any of the films I've just mentioned or any others I'm aware of. Mendes merely uses them as flavour in a hunter's stew of ingredients. What he's conjured up here is an entire hidden world, with its natives, its culture and its habits. It's certainly not for most but it's very much for some and that makes it a weird, cosmopolitan melting pot of dark subcultures. I adore it as a creation.

While Max remains our principal character throughout, with Harris and Charlie and a few others joining the fray, I should call out one more for special mention. She's Ming, the very savvy sixteen-year-old guide that Max acquires after he makes it into the city. She is an absolutely joyous character, carefully written and with a serious story arc. For all of the visual elements that I caught from various exploitation films, no exploitation filmmaker is going to be able to do this justice and especially not with a sixteen-year-old sidekick.

Outside of a smattering of spelling errors here and there, the most obvious downside to the book is the fact that it ends and I mean that both sincerely and in the sense that it also ends quickly and leaves us hanging. All we need to know for this book is there and the plot strands that should wrap up are resolved, so we shouldn't feel cheated, but it seems clear that Max's story doesn't end when the final

page is turned. There is obviously more to come, in a follow-up novel that S. C. Mendes has yet to write and I eagerly want to roll right on into that book without a gap. And I can't.

There are books by friends that I will not review, because I'm not going to put them through the embarrassment of me telling them how bad their work is. I'm going to review a lot of the better ones, for there are many of those too, in the coming months, now that I've reviewed my way through all 28 novels in the Humanx Commonwealth series by Alan Dean Foster, himself an Arizona author. I'm very happy that I started with this one, though, because it's going to be a stellar novel indeed that outdoes *The City*.

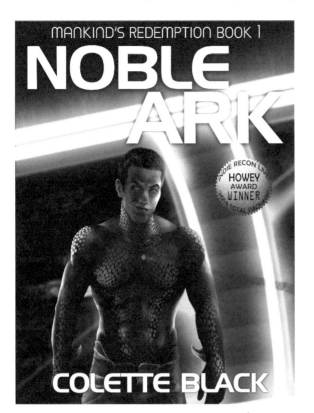

COLETTE BLACK

NOBLE ARK

MANKIND'S REDEMPTION #1

PUBLISHER:
DRAPUKAMO PUBLISHING
PUBLICATION DATE:
APRIL 2014

It's been five years since I read my first Colette Black, the realisation of that fact also serving to remind me just how long this one has sat on my TBR shelves. That was *Fourteen*, which I liked but which was also the opener to a trilogy that Black has not yet expanded. This also starts a trilogy, but I had picked up the second and third books at roughly the same time as the first, all three published before the release of *Fourteen*. I see that there's a fourth book that joined them earlier this year.

So it's about time that I read this one and, like *Fourteen*, it surprised me, if for different reasons.

Most obviously, this looks like a science fiction novel, with a traditionally futuristic font adorning the front cover and a back cover blurb about "parasitic aliens who consume human spinal fluid". The entire novel unfolds on the Noble Ark of the title, which is a spaceship carrying not only its usual array of goods but refugees from an attacked planet too. The lead characters are primarily Saeanians, the humans living on a colonised planet, and one Mwalgi. So yeah, surely it counts as science fiction?

Well, it does, but at heart this is really a romance novel, a genre I don't tend to read but which I can recognise when it shows up in other clothing. Should we strip away the setting in space in the future, we'd be left with a traditional love triangle with a taboo participant. Replace that setting with the antebellum deepsouth and Larkin Travgar, a half-Mwalgi, would become a mulatto, likely the illicit son of a slave and a plantation house lady, without the core story changing much at all.

If it was surprising to find this novel a romance clothed in sci-fi garb, it was also surprising to find how much I liked that. Certainly the progression isn't at all surprising but I was rooting for the leads all the way.

In this setting, the taboo is pretty blatant. The human race has spread out into the galaxy, though it seems as if it's a relatively recent expansion. We've encountered aliens and the Mwalgi have become our nemesis species. They see we humans as just livestock, not least because they need to consume our CSF, cerebro-spinal fluid. Now, this may be a remedy for a nutritional deficiency but most humans see it as a fix, making the Gis a species of addicts, animals driven by their urges.

That view is epitomised in Aline Taylor, a nineteen-year-old orphan under the care of Captain Trenoble of the Noble Ark. As you might well imagine, she's an orphan because Mwalgi raiders murdered her entire family and she hasn't forgotten. Mwalgi pirates are an occupational hazard for ships like the Noble Ark, so she trains for and looks forward to the next attack, so she can sneak out into the front lines, baiting them and killing as many as she can. She certainly considers them to be animals, at least until Lar shows up.

Larkin Trovgar arrives with a pirate ship but promptly turns on what Aline would consider his own kind, fighting alongside the humans and, with Aline, making all the difference in the battle. He's very good, carrying the title of Morten, meaning he's special forces, and Aline believes she has an honor debt to him because of what he does. That means that she fights to keep him out of the brig, where he'd be tortured and possibly killed, and in the

only place she can supervise him, her own quarters.

That doesn't make David happy and David's not just an ass but an entitled ass. He's from an important military family, he's a looker and he can turn on the charm. He could probably have almost any girl on board and rumours might suggest that he's already done so, but he wants Aline. When Lar shows up, he's been making good progress, from his perspective, and it's all a matter of time before he lands this conquest too, but Lar's an obstacle, who gradually becomes something else.

90% of the novel is taken up with what the final line of the back cover blurb promises us, namely, "As Larkin's presence brings out the best and worst in the human crew, and the Noble Ark is harassed by more Mwalgi ships, will Aline look past Larkin's alien heritage to find love, or will mistrust cost her everything?" I'm sure you can answer that supposedly rhetorical question right now without having read this novel.

What saves proceedings is that Black is a good writer, a very good writer for what is surely a self-published novel (it was published through Createspace by Drapukamo Publishing of Higley, AZ). Put simply, I cared about Aline and, to a little less of a degree, Lar. Just as importantly, I disliked David from the very outset and came to loathe him as things progress. I know those are the feelings Black wants me to have and I knew it after a few chapters, but she still had the job of bringing those feelings out of me and her writing did that well.

Part of it may be how patient this is. We can shout from the cheap seats at Aline for being overly naïve. We can shout at David for being a cad and sometimes hiss at him, too, when he's even more of an ass than usual. But we have to, because Aline has to learn for herself what's going on—nobody can tell her, even one of her close friends who likes her more than he can say—and David is clever enough to hide his darker side from her, if not from us. It takes a long while, but it has to and that depth of character makes this novel.

I also appreciated the early chapters, where Black sets up a new universe. I'd have liked a lot more exploration of human and Mwalgi interaction and some more about the political and socio-economic state of the galaxy, but maybe we'll see more of that in the succeeding books. For now, she sets up not merely characters, but introduces some culture, tech and even tactics too, from both sides. It's easily enough to ground us for now.

I did have a few issues, all relatively minor. There's some credulity stretching in how Lar is treated on board the Noble Ark, though Black does try not to stretch it too far. There's some plot convenience in how opinion starts to change, but it isn't outrageous. The one thing I didn't buy was the games, a traditional activity on board, not merely because of who gets to take part but because the scoring was contradictory and overly convenient.

I'm still wondering if Lar's accent is an issue to me or not. As a half-human, half-Mwalgi mostly fluent in English, Black keeps his alien origin apparent by giving him an accent. That makes sense, but he sometimes comes across as a French Yoda, which is far too ridiculous an image for us to take him quite as seriously as we should. Hopefully this diffuses over the following books, because he's far from stupid.

Another aspect that I'm unsure I'd consider an issue or not may tie to what audience Black was aiming for. Alina's nineteen and Lar, when translated into human years, is only a year older. I'm not sure about David, but he's not far adrift and that means that we have a young set of leads. That, and a focus on their respective relationships, makes this seem like YA and, at points, like a school story for kids. We're never at school, but it sometimes feels like we should be and that goes double during the games. That does jar a little with the more adult themes that come into play.

Overall, I'm happy that I finally got round to this novel as my Arizona book for the month and I'm eager to read on to see how things progress after the important changes at the end of this novel that I won't remotely spoil. The second book in the *Mankind's Redemption* series is *Desolation* and the third *Mwalgi Justice*, both of which are on my shelf at present. Book four, which I don't have, is *Lenfay's Hell*.

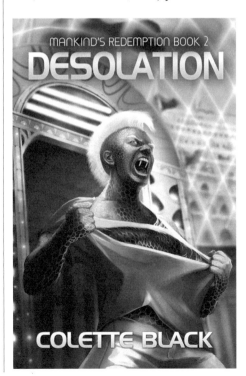

K. S. MERBETH

BITE

THE WASTELANDERS #1

PUBLISHER:
ORBIT BOOKS
PUBLICATION DATE:
JUL 2016

I met Kristyn Merbeth at TusCon last year and, while I couldn't afford to buy her books then and there, I ordered them online later. *Bite* is the first (of three) of them that I've read and, I believe, the first that she wrote. It was originally published as a mass market paperback by Orbit in 2016 but it's available now as half of a doorstop of a duology with *Raid*, collectively dubbed *The Wastelanders*.

As that might suggest, we're in an apocalyptic future, one that will feel notably familiar to anyone in the wastelander community (there are a lot of them here in state too) or to those who enjoy films like *Mad Max* or games like *Borderlands*. What's important is that it embraces many of their tropes, while taking a very different approach to the genre that I haven't quite seen before.

The first key thing to note is that time and place is consistently vague. We know that there was a civilisation and that it's fallen, but we're not once told that it's ours or, even if it is, where we happen to be or how far we got when this starts out. Some characters were certainly born before the nuclear war that wiped everything out, so it's recent, if not too recent. Our primary character is sixteen and she was born after. The technology available isn't beyond what we have today.

We never set foot in a city and we can only presume that they're all now in ruins. Instead, we're way out in the desert, where the radiation has done a different job to usual. It sends people insane and eventually kills them, but it doesn't turn them into mutants with melted skin and extra limbs. Maybe its most abiding impact is to massively increase the infant death rate, so it isn't a vastly populated desert and it won't become one any time soon.

Society has adapted pretty quickly, though, it seems. There are a bunch of small communities, populated by "townies" who stay where they are and try to carry on regardless in their new world. There are "traders" who travel around and barter for goods. There are "raiders", who simply prey on everyone else. And then there are "sharks", who murder people to sell their flesh as meat. Oh yeah, out here in the desolate wastes, cannibalism has made quite the comeback for anyone who runs out of cans of beans.

And, in the most overt departure from the standard post-apocalyptic tropes, a group of sharks make up our primary cast. Surely the biggest success Merbeth finds in this novel is to take people who would be usually seen as the bad guys, the outright villains of any other story and make them, if not entirely sympathetic, at least human beings with depth and history. None of them grew up wanting to be a shark or indeed became one overnight. There are stories here and we gradually hear them.

Another departure from the norm is to make this central band of sharks, well, a little stupid. Their leader is Wolf, who makes a lot of plans, none of which are well thought out or likely to succeed without a dose of blind luck. He's a big dreadlocked guy who would look right at home at a wasteland event, but for all his perceived callousness, he does have a heart and he's quickly a surrogate father for Kid. He's not a lovable rogue, as that cliché goes, but he is a rogue and he can be just a little lovable too.

Dolly is the matriarch of the group and she's an efficient killer, way up on any tough girl

chart, and she has the expected coloured hair. She also has a serious set of issues, inherited from a former job, and they've led her to be highly socially awkward. There's also a huge guy called Tank, who's sweet, even if he smells and likes to bash people's heads in; and Pretty Boy, who's just as good looking as his name suggests but is also a rank coward, ever ready to leave his colleagues in the lurch to hightail it out of anywhere fast.

And into this merry band of misfits comes Kid, because nobody uses their real name after the apocalypse, and she's far from the traditional heroine. For a start, she's only sixteen and very naïve, having grown up in a shelter with only her dad for company. She can't read,

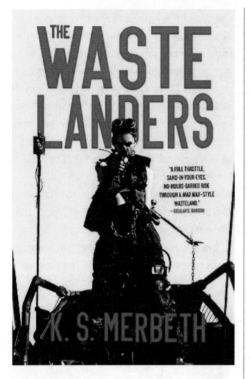

she can't shoot and she's very good at making stupid mistakes. At one point, she's given a grenade to throw so she does exactly that, not taking out the pin first. She also trusts far too easily for a world full of people willing to take whatever they can, but that humanises her and she soon becomes the humanising factor for this whole group.

As is befitting for Wolf's lack of coherent leadership, they don't set their own path so much as follow whatever path they can see at any particular time. For characters who firmly believe that they're the masters of their own destinies, they're buffeted on the radioactive wind of fate with abandon and they have a knack of finding trouble wherever that wind takes them. They're also good at being the wildcards who will shake up whatever that trouble might be, very likely making it worse

in the process.

If Kid humanises them, then the ineptitude they exude from every pore, which sometimes borders on the slapstick, renders them a little endearing. There's one crucial point where they're on the run and so need to adopt fake personae to get safely into a community. They are all on board with the idea and they dress up a bit, but they're in by the time they realise that not one of them actually selected a new name and so now they need to pretend on the fly. The humour here is as black as you might expect, but it's also sometimes laugh out loud funny.

I liked this a lot. It works as a ripping yarn, a B movie wasteland with guns and trucks in (over)abundance; suitably wild raiders outshining the bland townies; and only a couple of plot conveniences, neither of which grates much. It works better as a character study, an attempt to explore the old maxim that every villain is a hero in their own story, so turning the genre on its head. And it works as simply a piece of prose, with mature writing neatly disguised as an action movie.

My most common responses to this novel were to keep on turning pages, because its telling in the present tense adds serious urgency to the story, and to grin a lot at whatever wildly unrecommended antics Wolf and his crew have got up to next. There were telling points, however, where I also put the book down for a moment so I could admire a paragraph or a turn of phrase.

The first one was when Dolly returns Kid's beanie after an incident. Kid's response is to rush up to her and hug her, which takes the social awkward Dolly very much aback, but she recovers her mental balance by shooting a bad guy in the face. The juxtaposition of such wildly different emotions is handled perfectly. Another example follows a downpoint in the interpersonal relationships of Wolf's crew. Kid explains her reaction: "I stare at my feet. The silence feels thick, and I'm struck by the impression that all of them are strangers again."

For a post-apocalyptic novel that doesn't at all care about its apocalypse, just the charact-ers who survive it, this is a heck of a lot of throwaway fun but it's also elevated by its experimental convention-flouting and by its touching characterisation. I look forward to *Raid*, which I believe is set within the same wasteland but with a focus on different characters, leaving our new shark friends for what I'm sure is a memorable cameo.

K. S. MERBETH

RAID

THE WASTELANDERS #2

PUBLISHER:
ORBIT BOOKS

PUBLICATION DATE:
JULY 2017

I have so many signed books on my shelf by Arizona authors that I really don't want to repeat myself a lot in my monthly attempt to catch up with them all. However, I'm returning to K. S. Merbeth for three reasons. For one, it's been six months since I reviewed her debut novel, *Bite*, to which this is a sequel. For another, I thoroughly enjoyed its take on the post-apocalypse, which was at once entirely what we expect and something completely new. And third, my copy of *Raid* is the second half of a doorstep of a volume, following *Bite* in a behemoth called *The Wastelanders*. Being able to move this off of my headboard means I can put at least three or four other books there instead.

When I said that this is a sequel, I was technically telling the truth, but misleading just a little. It's not a direct sequel, a continuation of the misadventures of Wolf and his crew of sharks. This is set in the same world, with a new leading lady, a new set of characters and a new story that eventually leads us to the time and place where *Bite* ends, so that we can revisit with Wolf and his mob and continue both stories forward.

Some things are very much the same. This is once more told in the first person and present tense, the combination appropriate for the post-apocalypse, as it keeps everything urgent and immediate. The initial setting is the eastern wastes, rather than the western ones, but it contains the same sort of people who are struggling to survive in the same sort of ways. Over in the east, the raider chief is a legend of a man, Jedediah Johnson, but he dominates in the same way that the Saint did in the west.

Another similarity is that I think it's safe to say that the bad guys are the heroes again, but not remotely to the same degree. Our lead is Clementine, who's a bounty hunter who kind of likes to kill people. That's not a traditional hero, even after the end of the world, but there are reasons why she does what she does and they're fair enough. Also, she has rules, somewhat like Dexter's rules and given to her early on in her life, again like Dexter. She has a mission and it isn't particularly far into the book when we hear it said. "I need people to know it was me. I need to be the woman who freed the eastern wastes."

Of course, the way she'll do that is to take down Jedediah Johnson, the man who burned her town and killed her family, and she's handed him on a platter. Alex the Collector

has an informant, who says that there's an escape tunnel leading right into Johnson's room in his mansion in Wormwood. Clementine has her doubts, but in a fantastic segue, we go from one chapter ending with her not believing it at all to a new one beginning, "The tunnel is real." Sure enough, in she goes and out she comes again with a rather surprised and surprisingly young prisoner.

The problem is that Alex the Collector won't take him. He's too big a name with too scary a reputation and too tough a crew and, if he pays his bounty, Johnson's men will destroy him utterly in revenge. So the only thing for it is for Clementine to take the legendary Jedediah Johnson on a road trip over the desert to the western wastes and deliver him to the Saint, who's broadcasting over the radio that he's cleaning up the wastelands and paying bounties for this sort of bad guy.

I'd say that the real story starts here, as Clementine hits the road in Alex's car with Johnson bound on the floorboards, headed west. Then again, that's up for debate. Readers of *Bite* know what happens to Saint and, sure enough, Clementine arrives at Shark's tower just in time to see it empty of raiders, now that the great man has been toppled. So much for that plan. So maybe the real story begins then. Or maybe... no, I'll shut up now.

Let's just say that rather a lot happens on the way to Saint's tower and quite a lot more happens after it and all of it helps build this story. I mentioned similarities to *Bite* above, but there are notable differences too. Most obviously, Clementine is a kick-ass lead. I do think I like Kid a little more, but it's fair to say that the story of *Bite* happened around her. She's a mouse learning not to be as much of a mouse. If there's a word that describes Clementine worse than "mouse", I'm not sure it would be. She takes the story by the balls and head-butts it in the teeth. She's the architect of her own destiny and I think her story arc is the opposite to Kid's. Kid is a soft girl who has to learn how to be tough. In many ways, Clementine is a tough girl who has to learn how to be soft. At least, sometimes.

I'll also mention Cat and Bird, as they're a perfect example of something that could have been derivative but isn't derivative. They're another couple of bounty hunters who know Clementine well and bump into her on the road, but they have a repetition thing going, where Cat will say something and Bird, quite obviously a damaged human being, will echo it. I immediately thought of the pair of rogue plumbers in *Brazil* but it's common enough a trope that I saw it again last night in the form of a pair of old sisters in an episode of *The Memoirs of Sherlock Holmes*. However, as always, Merbeth adds a twist, in this instance Bird being afraid of seeing her own skin. That's new and very cool.

What I won't mention is pretty much everything else because it would be very easy to spoil this book and I don't want to do that. If you've read *Bite*, you'll be expecting a pair of things once the direction of *Raid* is set: that Clementine isn't going to get her bounty from Saint because Saint's not going to be alive when or if she gets to him and that Wolf and his crew are going to show up for at least a cameo. I'll happily tell you that you're right on both of those fronts, but I won't tell you anything else. I think you deserve to experience these twists and turns on your own, because they're handled adroitly, not least due to the book only containing two primary characters.

And that's it for the Wastelanders, it seems,

at least as far as novels go. There is a short story called *Pretty Vicious* that came out in between these two books, which explores the back story of Dolly, the socially awkward matriarch of Wolf's crew. I haven't read it, but I should, even though I know it's likely to be the last thing I'll be able to read from this post-apocalyptic world. Merbeth has moved on and up to a space opera series, *Nova Vita Protocol* published by Kristyn Merbeth and beginning with the 2019 novel *Fortuna*. I have the first two and the third is due this year and I'm really looking forward to seeing how her style works in a very different genre.

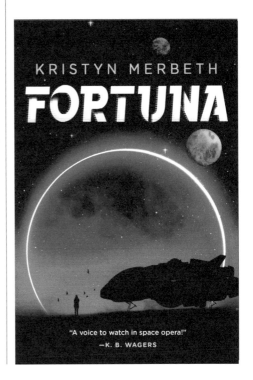

BRUCE DAVIS

PLATINUM MAGIC

MAGIC LAW #1

PUBLISHER:
BRICK CAVE MEDIA
PUBLICATION DATE:
JANUARY 2018

So many urban fantasy novels merge our world and a supernatural one, of elves and orcs and whatever else. Bruce Davis does that here too, but in an original way indeed. We're the alien dimension, for a change, and nobody here sets a single foot on our side, but there is a very neat connection that left a big smile on my face.

This is an alien world, we might say, a sort of parallel universe; but it isn't really a science fiction novel. It's a fantasy novel because this is clearly a fantasy world in which the fantasy species are intermingled and everything runs on magic. However, because fantasy is a highly versatile genre, this is also a cop thriller even if Simon Buckley and Haldron Stonebender are technically King's Agents based in a city called

Cymbeline and the reason behind Hal's name is that he's a dwarf.They find themselves quickly in trouble, because their kind of legal raid on a cottage they expect to be a bomb making factory run by orc terrorists ends up with a high elf dead at their hands. Sure, she was trying to kill Hal at the time, she had a slew of animated golems running around (illegal outside a laboratory) and she was about to sacrifice an orc in a blood ritual; but she's also quickly discovered to be a college professor, Glendowyn High-tower, the sister of the Steward of Tintagel, so her death is also an international incident.

I liked this from moment one and for a lot of reasons.

One is simply that I'd like to see a lot more

novels using the sort of setting we see more often on-screen in TV shows like *Alien Nation* or films like the recent Netflix original, *Bright*. I haven't read anything in this sort of vein since last May, when I reviewed Dan Stout's *Titanshade*, and I'm struggling to think of the time before that.

Another is that Bruce Davis does a fantastic job of worldbuilding. This isn't a large book, running only three hundred pages in an oddly wide font, but he somehow gives us history and science without ever diverting away from his characters and the quest that they have at hand. I'd love to read more books set in this world, even if they don't feature these characters, because it's a rich one indeed.

The history is delicately inserted, because Davis has no interest in turning a novel full of action into an academic exercise in the way that Tolkien did on occasion, but it's highly evocative. The tyranny of the Magisterium is gone, with a new, more open world following the Commonwealth Accords. Now, each of the races seems to get on well with this other one and maybe a little with that one too but not that one over there, with those permutations changing depending on which one we happen to be talking about. And the backdrop is of a terrorist threat from the Azeris, driven from a neighbouring country.

The science is delicately inserted too, as it could easily have become a distraction. Suffice it to say that, while all the tech runs on magic, with any King's Agent breaching squad having a Fire Mage ready for use, that magic behaves according to fundamental scientific principles. Spells are cast and contained in machinery, whether that's colourfully named weaponry or the magic mirrors that function as phones or computer monitors do for us.

You won't need to know anything about quantum theory or probability matrices to enjoy this novel, just acknowledge that there are rigid boundaries around what's possible in this world. You can't just wish for something and wham, it shows up, and, quite frankly, that's a good thing. It grounds this novel in reality, even if it isn't our reality.

Another obvious reason to enjoy this book is because Haldron Stonebender goes by Hal and I'm automatically a fan of every novel that features a primary character named Hal. This particular Hal doesn't wear a kilt and isn't likely to be based on me (I may be equally as stubborn but I've never had an issue with orcs), but he's still a Hal and that's cool.

A wider reason to dig the book is that it unfolds not just like a cop show but like a film noir cop show. The cottage that Simon and Hal

115

breach early may or may not also be involved with Azeri bomb-makers and they'll pursue the line of inquiry because they're professionals, but the presence of a high elf doing blood magic spins them into another investigation, one watched by a representative of the elves very carefully indeed.

So, what we really have here are potentially two stories, which may or may not be linked, and a third wheel for our leads to work around. She's an elf, a Gray Ranger at that, Sylvie Graystorm, which makes her just as dangerous as her surname suggests and she's, another worthy character. And, while none of these are PIs, they have to follow an uncertain and dangerous trail without much coordination with their departments, because the higher ups are too busy with politics and are likely to shut down anything they suggest.

So, lots of reasons to read this. How about reasons not to read this? Well, I can't come up with too many. I'm not a big fan of the font and the book is a little heavy for only three hundred pages, but shrug. That's all I can muster for negatives. The cover's fantastic and the contents are even better. Right now, moguls should be arguing about how much they want to spend on the TV show adaptation and who to cast in multi-species roles.

And I want, not a sequel per se, but more books set in this world, hopefully but not necessarily featuring these characters. There's a lot more to tell us and I look forward to listening.

BRUCE DAVIS

GOLD MAGIC

MAGIC LAW #2

PUBLISHER:
BRICK CAVE MEDIA

PUBLICATION DATE:
JUNE 2020

I've liked Bruce Davis for years, because he's a gentlemen to sell books beside at conventions; and he's a level headed debater and a fascinating panelist who can speak on varied topics. I've liked him all the more since I read *Platinum Magic*, the first book in his *Magic Law* series, which I reviewed at the Nameless Zine last year.

This is the second and it does much the same thing; throwing the lead characters from that book, if they're still alive, into a new case that's just as high-reaching and just as important. It cuts down a little on the worldbuilding, having established a general history as background, and it cuts down a little on the science too, now that we have a grasp on the fact that there are rules that govern the use of magic in this world in place of, say, electricity. There's also no further connection to our own world, which was an intriguing little moment in the first book but seems to be left as that.

While it would seem to be a good idea to read *Platinum Magic* first, to gain from its snippets of worldbuilding and science and its introduction of the central cast, I don't feel like it's necessary as this ought to work well as a standalone. You could start here and easily grasp everything you need to take you all the way through the novel.

Our protagonist is again Simon Buckley, a capable and honest King's Agent (translation: cop) in the multi-species city of Cymbeline, though his team has changed since the prior book. Haldron Stonebender, a dwarf, is still his sidekick and mentor. Liam Aster, the human fire mage was new last time out but is now settled. The new fish this time is Kermal Brackenville, a half orc. Also, while she isn't part of the team proper, I should mention Simon's girlfriend, Sylvie Graystorm, an elf working as a Gray Ranger (translation: cop) in the neighbouring Havens, because she joins them for quite a while this time out, too.

The spark for this case is the discovery of four dead orc children in the Hollows, one of the roughest parts of Cymbeline and the one with the highest orc population, many of them Azeri refugees from the south. It's the sort of crime that might go unreported and likely underinvestigated, except that it features a ritual element. Magic was done here, blood magic, and that brings it to the attention of Buckley. Suffice it to say that it expands from there in many different directions, each of which has a particular resonance within this world.

Anything that directly affects the orcs is a political football, as they occupy the lowest rung of the ladder in the Commonwealth; even though each of the species is supposedly equal in stature, following the Accords. Davis does explore racism as a concept here, including within Buckley's team though it's dealt with easier there, but he explores more orc culture, which is fascinating and only likely to become more so in future books, given how certain characters fit within that culture. In particular, the Hollows has an awkward balance of underworld power and that's shaken massively during this book, enough that we know it's not going to be remotely the same next time out.

Anything that incriminates the elves is a political football too, as their society is long established and relatively rigid, with a firm respect for status and position, whether it's earned or not. It may be fair to mention here that Sylvie comes from a noble line, her father seated on the Council, but she's incurred the wrath of the family for working in law enforcement and she's given up all rights to her particular title.

It's not difficult to see the humans of the Commonwealth as Americans, with orcs representing an ethnic minority, perhaps African or Italian Americans, and the elves representing the British. I'm not sure how the dwarves fit into that overly simplified translation, as they feel more Viking than Native American. Of course, Davis probably never meant for us to attempt to pigeonhole like this and may not have set these species in these particular places in his world with any such translation in mind.

And, of course, anything that might cast a bad light on the Peacekeepers, this world's equivalent of the boys-in-blue, is a political football as well; and a touchy one given the events of the previous book. Buckley makes slow and steady progress, of course, in trying to figure out what these four dead orc kids represent, why and for what blood magic was performed and to where the path that opens up is going to lead, but this case isn't a straight line. Things happen in reaction to his discoveries and those grow in importance as the story runs on.

It doesn't help that Princess Rebeka Fangbern, one and only daughter of King Thorsten Fangbern, seems to be a regular at Lily's Place too, the pub outside which the four bodies were found. She isn't under any suspicion for the crime, but there has to be a reason why she's in the Hollows and that's not at all obvious. The only thing that is obvious is that someone of her stature showing up in the story (and the Hollows generally) is going to generate some serious ramifications and, sure enough, it does.

I liked this a lot. This world was new to me,

and all readers, in *Platinum Magic*, but it felt vibrant, fleshed-out and unusual. My initial thought was that it ought to be adapted into a TV show, which may be a common response to many books by many readers but rarely is from me. Television loves cop shows and the more unusual their settings, the better they seem to do. This would seem to be an unusual setting indeed but not an unprecedented one, given Netflix's *Bright*. The ideas in that were great but the writing wasn't as good as it is here. Davis may have come to this as a writer of science fiction, but he's a natural for cop dramas too.

Having devoured this second book in the series, I'm still on board with a TV version, but it's fair to say that these books should occupy a season each. Davis isn't interested in merely churning out another case per book with his characters static in the foreground. Each of them has their own journey and that means that the make-up of the central cast is going to change more frequently than television tends to prefer. Also, with a book a season, he'll have time to write new books rapidly enough to not find himself lagging behind pesky production schedules. After all, these only run 250 pages or so, as much as he manages to fit into them.

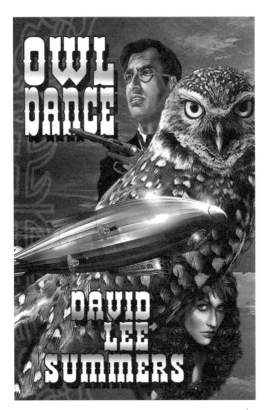

DAVID LEE SUMMERS

OWL DANCE

CLOCKWORK LEGION #1

PUBLISHER:
SKY WARRIOR BOOKS
PUBLICATION DATE:
SEPTEMBER 2011

Ever since I started deliberately reviewing an Arizona novel every month, I knew I would be getting round to this one sooner rather than later. David Lee Summers may technically live in New Mexico, but he works in Arizona, as an astronomer at Kitt Peak National Observatory, and he's a regular at local science fiction and steampunk conventions here in state who gives excellent panel. He's also a real gentleman and a good writer and I own far more of his books than I've read.

Owl Dance is one of those that I've read before, though it's been a long time, but, after expanding a couple of short stories into this fixup novel, he's continued that expansion into a *Clockwork Legion* series, which currently numbers four books, and I've been looking forward to reading the rest for a long time.

After all, they're weird westerns, they continually subvert expectations and they feature a full bingo card of all the coolest things that should be in weird westerns that continually subvert expectations.

This one is set in 1876 in what was then the New Mexico Territory and it features a pair of leads who were far from the norm in 2011. Ramon Morales isn't merely a Latino lead, he starts out the novel as the Sheriff of the town of Socorro, even if he's forced to abandon that office within a single chapter. His co-lead, who naturally also becomes his love interest, is a Persian lady, Fatemeh Karimi, who's in the New World to make a new start, having escaped the oppression of her homeland. She's seen as a witch, a bruja, though she's really a curandera, or healing woman. He's Roman

Catholic and she is of the Bahá'í faith. And, as far as I'm concerned, every aspect of that is another detail that makes this book worthier.

I believe their saga started in a short story, *The Persian Witch*, and that's what kicks off this novel. Each chapter has a title, but there are no contents, which highlights how this is a fixup novel rather than a collection of short stories. Initially, it seems more like the latter because, beyond a vague progression forward for Ramon and Fatemeh, each chapter feels like a standalone. Only as the novel starts to really pick up speed do we start to see how the early chapters are origin stories for different characters, who start to increasingly interweave as the plot runs on. Before long, they start to feel like chapters and we don't want to put the book down in case we miss something.

For those wondering about that bingo card of coolness, I should introduce some of those characters, starting with Legion, an incredibly old nanite swarm who has been wandering through space on a quest to learn how intelligent life evolves. I did tell you that this was a weird western, right? Some relatively unconvincing psychohistory by Legion later, there's Gen. Alexander Gorloff of the Russian Empire, who serves as the villain of the piece, albeit a villain who epitomises the concept that every villain is a hero in his own story.

There's a genial mad scientist by the name of Prof. M. K. Maravilla, who earns his place in the large pantheon of worthy steampunk mad scientists. There's an unusual band of gentleman pirates under the command of Onofre Cisneros, who are raiding ships off California. There's an obnoxious young gunslinger called Billy McCarty, who has some growing to do but is certainly given an opportunity. And, last but not least, there's a proficient female bounty hunter fabulously named Larissa Crimson. All these and more play out their roles in this tangled web of steampunk shenanigans.

The core of the conflict lies in Legion's assumption that it's simply inevitable that the young nation of America will grow up to rival the Russian Empire, thus nuclear showdowns in the Cold War, which is a bit of a stretch, but it prompts the nanite swarm to fix that in advance by giving the Russians a glimpse of airship technology and having them invade. It'll save the world. As you can imagine, the American army and a whole host of characters, who are not limited to those above, find ways to get included in the war effort.

It's hard not to like this from the outset. While Summers refuses to engage full gear until very late in the novel, there's plenty of action throughout, from the witch hunt which prompts our heroes to get the heck out of Socorro to the owl dance of the title, which features some cool flying machines in battle with the gigantic airships of the Russian Empire. Every time we blink, there's another neat character to keep the cast expanding, and they all get something to do, even if it doesn't seem like it at the time. The plot strands are woven with care into the novel at large.

The language finds an odd compromise between the verbose and overly descriptive fashion of many Victorian novels and the rip-roaring pulp style of the thirties. It's not verbose enough to fit among the former but too deliberate to fit among the latter. I think that's deliberate and it plays well but feels maybe a little too matter-of-fact for something that features so many elements that are weird and wonderful for the era. Maybe Summers could have shifted a little closer to the pulp style, so we turn the pages quicker to find the next thrill but enjoy just as much.

The characters are a lot of fun. The core duo share a fantastic dynamic, which promises to be one of the highlights of future books. It's fun seeing how different they are in so many ways, even though Fatemeh is above mere culture shock, but so similar in others. The rest of the ensemble cast aren't merely supporting characters but ones who would earn "guest credits" for the name actors who would bring them to life in what would be a glorious TV series because they're co-stars in their own episodes. The real supporting characters are historical figures like scientist Dimitri Mendeleev and Czar Alexander II of Russia. I look forward to American equivalents in future novels.

What I like most about this, though, is how it continually subverts expectations. Fone example, there's a chapter titled *The Clockwork Lobo*, which is indeed about a clockwork wolf and therefore we're already on board with what it's going to be doing. It doesn't. It has a completely different purpose and it's a worthy one which highlights how Summers is as much a scientist as a writer. The pirates of California are the best example. We know exactly how pirates function in steampunk novels and we look forward to another runthrough of the same 'ol, same' ol, only to discover that he simply doesn't want to go there. Again, he has another purpose for these pirates that pays off later in the novel. Some may be frustrated by his cheating us of what we expect, but I see his subversion of the genre norms as my personal highlight of the novel.

And, yes, I'm sure that's just as deliberate as his unusual choice of characters and the ways by which he weaves owls into the narrative whenever he can. Fatemeh has the ability to talk with owls, a sort of superpower that aids her and Ramon at a few points in the book. Others see owls in a mystical or mythical light, like the Russians who remember how an owl saved Genghis Khan so are treated as symbols of great power. Sometimes this feels a little forced, but it's good to see the theming.

With a brief note of praise for the subtle way in which Summers handles the racism of the era and a nod to all the discovery that goes on as a commentary on the era, from submarines to airships via a game of baseball, I'll wrap up by looking forward to the second book.

This saw print in 2011, making it an early David Lee Summers. *Lightning Wolves* followed it in 2014, when he had a lot more work under his belt, so I'm expecting it to share the same successes but also ride a little smoother. Later books, *The Brazen Shark* and *Owl Riders* arrived on a two year cycle, which makes me wonder if it has wrapped up with four volumes or whether the year from hell delayed book five. Let's find out!

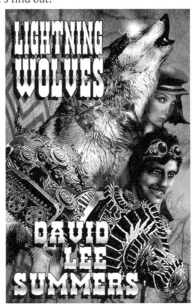

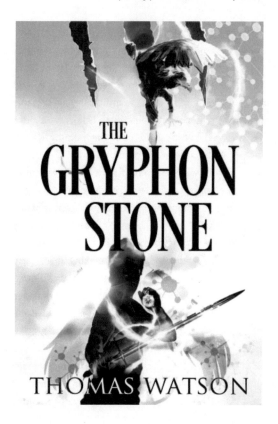

THOMAS WATSON

THE GRYPHON STONE

PUBLISHER:
DESERT STARS PUBLISHING

PUBLICATION DATE:
NOVEMBER 2017

Thomas Watson is a great example of why I needed to start this Arizona author project a lot sooner than I did. I've enjoyed both his company and his panels at quite a variety of conventions and I've picked up a stack of his books over that time. But I hadn't read any of them until now.

The Gryphon Stone is a recent book, compared to the others I have, published in 2017, after each of the five volumes of his *War of the Iteration* series, but it's also a standalone and so seemed like a better place to start. It also has a better cover, which is hardly a gimme but it never hurts. This one's an engaging cover that somehow hints at what might be inside without leaving us sure of anything, even the genre.

I have to admit to a sinking feeling when I opened the cover, because this falls for some of the more easily fixable problems of self-published or small press books. The proofing is bad enough that it failed on the table of contents and the text is left aligned instead of being justified the way the laws of nature require. However, I've been found myself in this spot before with an Arizona author (hello, Michael Bradley) who failed in putting a pair of books into print the way they should have been but succeeded nonetheless in telling an excellent set of stories within them. So, let's move on.

I'm not sure how far I managed to get into *The Gryphon Stone* before Watson hooked me, but it wasn't far. The first few chapters were good but a little work because he had a lot of worldbuilding to do and it overwhelmed the story somewhat. Not enough for me to leave, I should add, but enough for me to put the book down for the night and think about it before picking it up again the next evening.

I'll try to compress all that admirable detail for the sake of a brief synopsis. This is part of the autobiography of David K. Render, a formerly retired colonel in the U.N.M.S., the United Nations Multiverse Survey. He spent a great deal of quality time on an alternate Earth called Adrathea in partnership with Treyvar Olvanak of the Alvehn, but he has no wish to go back there ever again.

There are multiple reasons but one overrides all the others. He once met and fell in love with an Adrathean lady but the time slips that often creep in between the worlds made a simple trip home turn into a journey of generations, so that her heartbreak when he failed to return became literally a thing of legend, retold in a popular tragic ballad, an awkward concept for Render but a very cool one for us that I haven't encountered in any similarly-framed book.

But Treyvar comes to see him and ask him to go back anyway and he knows that he must. There's business undone and he has a part in it. Treyvar is a member of a very advanced civilisation, who are friends and partners to humans, but a side effect of their civility is that they're physically unable to kill another Alvehn and, indeed, Treyvar stopped David from killing a particular Alvehn in the past. And now, that same Alvehn, Edren by name, is wreaking havoc on Adrathea, usurping the throne from King Parick's descendants who lived and died over generations while David farmed for a few years in Williams, AZ.

We learn all this in only a few pages, while Watson also introduces us to the technology of navigating between the worlds, the reasons why Adrathea is perpetually stuck almost into an industrial revolution and a whole bunch of other background details. This is all cool but it's a lot to take in so quickly, especially as it's science fiction and we suddenly find ourselves in what feels like a fantasy novel after Trayvar and Render travel through a Stabilized Rip Station, to Adrathea.

At this point, the book felt decent and full of promise, but I'd taken maybe three nights to get half a dozen chapters in. Which is fine. But once I got just a little bit further in, I was unable to put this book down and I found myself finishing it at five in the morning because I didn't want to miss a word. Oh yes, it got that immersive!

It also got that emotional and I should build to the reasons why. I liked how the fantasy unfolded from the start. Those Adratheans who knew Render in the old days are all long dead, but I liked that he's recognisable as a figure of legend himself, not just from that tragic ballad but on his own merits. He fought hard and well for Adrathea and they have remembered him as Daffyd the Outworlder.

I liked how they find a companion, Sidraytha Condor Voriss, a warrior from the Isles of Wulde. I liked how she and Render, as people not easily recognised, travel into the city of Morvain and attract trouble, learning plenty as they went. I liked how Render freed a gryphon from captivity on the road into town, because he's a hero and it was the right thing to do. I liked how Sid ends up with a magic sword at the university that she must be destined to receive. It's not really magic, of course, just Alvehn technology, but you get the picture. I liked a lot of things here and somewhere in there Watson hooked me.

What made me absolutely not put the book down was the way he worked emotion. Not too far into the book, Daffyd, Sid and Trayvar are on a train, travelling from somewhere to somewhere else in search of the lost prince of the realm, who's presumably alive but in hiding, working as muscle as they do so. And they're attacked. They fight and the boy who's been awkwardly pursuing Sid is killed while saving her life. And, excuse me while I collect myself, three weeks after reading this section, before I continue.

She goes berserker and shocks everyone in a piece of magnificent writing. Her religious beliefs have her mount a vigil in his honour, throughout the night. She does this out in the wilds, back to back with Daffyd and their swords between them. It remains silent up to dawn, at which point they get up to find the entire caravan sitting there silently in a neat gesture of respect. They've sat there all night. I don't want to overplay this, because it isn't entirely surprising, but the sheer majesty of Watson's writing in this section is palpable. It's been a while since an author has conjured tears from me like this.

And, what's more, the bugger did it again, later, in a scene I won't spoil but which I saw coming whole chapters earlier. I knew exactly what was going to go down, almost to the detail, and he got me again anyway. Sure, Watson can build worlds, craft characters and recount action as if he's been doing it for decades. He's a good writer in all those ways. But, when it comes to rooking us between the eyes with scenes of real emotion, he's as great as anyone I've read in a long, long time. And I don't just mean local Arizona authors. I mean

period.

And, frankly, I ought to stop there because you really don't need to know any more. You don't need to know how well this merges the twin genres of science fiction and fantasy or how the copious amounts of intrigue and romance pans out. You don't even need to know about the gryphons and how they have long partnered with the Adratheans, using the Gryphon Stone of the title, that partnership damaged by Edren's shenanigans as the despotical Regent. It would all help to sell you on the book, but you don't need that.

Just trust me about the way Watson handles emotion. You've read plenty of my reviews, enough to know that I don't often indulge in hyperbole, bt I'll do it here. I'm tearing up just remembering how these scenes went down and it's three weeks since I read this novel. Frankly, that's enough of a recommendation right there.

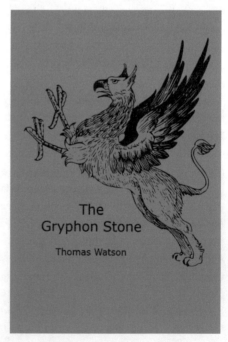

ETHAN RUSSELL ERWAY

MICHAEL BELMONT AND
THE TOMB OF ANUBIS

MICHAEL BELMONT #1

PUBLISHER:
UNKNOWN

PUBLICATION DATE:
NOV 2011

You know, I think I must have had this book for about a decade. Ethan Erway was one of the authors selling his books at the first events I appeared at and I think I bought this one before that, at a Phoenix Comicon shortly after it moved to Phoenix, drawn in by the cover and sold by the idea. It's therefore a prime candidate to check out as one of my monthly reviews of books written by Arizona authors, because I'm way overdue with it.

The good news is that I enjoyed it a great deal. It's a pulp adventure story, but written very specifically for and about kids. There are adults in this novel, some of them intriguing and others not so much, but they're never the focus of the story. It's always about Michael Belmont and his cohorts, who are not very old.

I don't believe Erway tells us, probably very deliberately, exactly how old they are (if he did, I didn't note it down) but I got the impression that Michael is either young teenager or he's about to be, while his sister Abigail is a little younger. They live in Prescott, Arizona, but Michael's best friend, Liam MacDonald, lives in a bona fide Scottish castle, outside a village called Tarbet, which is a real place on the western shores of Loch Lomond.

"Wouldn't that be cool!", I hear you saying, and Erway's relish for this sort of unrealistic but undeniably cool detail is the main reason why this worked for me. It feels in many ways like a novel written by a British author in the early decades of the last century, aided by the odd approach to have none of these kids see technology as inherent to their ability to live their lives. I don't think any of them even have phones and their instincts are far more to go outside and investigate the fairy ring up the hillside than to sit down and watch YouTube or play a videogame. They even read, for goodness sakes, and, while I enjoyed the sheer nostalgic thrill, this may feel anachronistic to some readers.

Certainly we're not in 1920 because the kids get more places by plane than they do by car—they sure do fly a lot!—and the numerous pop culture references dotted throughout the book like Easter eggs on a DVD are not from silent movies. Liam gets called a "scruffy little nerf-herder" at one point, by a Scottish fairy of all things, who's apparently seen *Star Wars*, and the collection on display in a concealed wing of McGinty Castle has an Infinity Gauntlet, though it's not called that here, of course. Kudos for that, by the way, given that this came out in 2011, so before *The Avengers*, let alone *Infinity War*, so it's a comic book reference rather than a movie one. That in itself echoes my previous paragraph, though there's a Tobor here too.

And I just let slip another unrealistic but undeniably cool detail! Not only does Liam live in a Scottish castle, but it has its very own secret wing accessed by a secret corridor and a collection of really cool stuff for these kids to discover and explore, while out in the countryside around the castle is a frolic of fairies in a fairy grove and a... but, no, I'm getting ahead of myself. Much of the joy here is in figuring out what other unrealistic but undeniably cool detail Erway is going to slip in a chapter or two from now before the kids do, so I'm not going to spoil any more of those surprises.

Of course, given the title of the book and the beautiful cover art by Steph Roman, we know we're not going to be exploring Scotland with the kids for long and they're going to end up catching a plane over to Egypt, which is where their parents are. Here I should explain that Michael's and Abby's father is a cultural anthropologist and their mother is an archaeologist. Liam's father is a historian who buys and sells artifacts and was introduced to the Belmont family by Michael's Uncle Link, who owns an antique store in Sedona and is clearly something more than that too, from the first moment he shows up in the story.

The spark for the Egyptian story, though, is Liam's great uncle Shamus, an adventurous spirit who managed to vanish without a trace seventeen years earlier. He was in Egypt, helping to map a necropolis being excavated in the desert west of Edfu, as an expert in archaeological cartography, when it was closed down following a set of mysterious deaths. He's believed to have snuck back in and somehow died inside the necropolis, though his body was never found. Now the Egyptian government is opening it back up again and the Belmonts are going to work there, leaving the kids with Liam's family at McGinty Castle.

But, you will, no doubt, be shocked to discover that they stumble onto things in Scotland that have a direct bearing on what's going on in Egypt and are gradually trawled into the heart of the mystery of which the adults seem to be blissfully unaware—or at least notably dismissive of, because, hey, they're scientists and they're not going to fall for a story that sounds like it could have been a *Scooby-Doo* episode. And so it falls to the kids to solve the case and save the day, while continuing to discover new unrealistic but undeniably cool details. This novel may not stand up to much analysis but it's a heck of a lot of fun and I wish I'd have been able to read this at the age of seven or eight. Had I done so, it would surely have become a favourite.

Of course, I'm not a seven- or eight-year-old kid now, so it's easy to see past the wonders that Erway obviously enjoys hurling our way and find the flaws. In fact, some are pretty clear when opening the cover, including the design choices because this is yet another self-published Arizona novel and Erway makes a few of the usual mistakes. For a start, the text isn't justified, though the layout is admittedly neat and tidy, with a good font, decent line spacing and appropriate indents. There's almost no use of smart quotes, though they do creep in at points, and ALL EMPHASIS IS MADE THROUGH USE OF CAPITALS, which is just obnoxious. Given the subject matter, I guess I can forgive Erway for using Papyrus for his headers and chapter titles but I surely hope he wouldn't be quite that clichéd today. There are multiple editions, so I'd also hope he fixed the other things raised in this paragraph too.

Delving into content, there are some overt plot conveniences but no more than you'd expect in an adventure novel for kids. My only real moment of concern arrived as the story started to explain what the Egyptian gods actually were because, while it's an interesting idea, it's also a problematic one for cultural reasons. It never becomes an actual problem here, but it could well do as the series runs on, if it keeps them in focus. Book two is called *Michael Belmont and the Heir of Van Helsing*, the famous vampire hunter being mentioned here if not actually present as a character. Then it's *Michael Belmont and the Curse of the Thunderbird*, so it seems that Erway is moving between cultures, which is easy to do when your char-

acters fly as much as these.

To sum up, I have to say that I had a blast with this. I'd happily recommend it to any kid with a nascent sense of adventure, because it nails that mindset wonderfully. The older that kid gets, the less they're going to feel an aura of wonder infused into the story, but an older reader who read this sort of material when they were kids should get a strong whiff of nostalgia from it. It's frankly riddled with of undeniably cool things and they're a lot more important to any kid or any adult remembering when they were any kid than the unrealistic side. It runs three hundred pages and, when I turned the last one, I wanted to keep on going into book two. If there's a better recommendation than that, I don't know what it would be.

DARRYL DAWSON

IF IT BLEEDS

PUBLISHER:
NIGHTSHADE PUBLICATIONS
PUBLICATION DATE:
JUNE 2019

I knew exactly how much COVID impacted my life when I realised that Darryl Dawson has a new novella out; it's been out for almost two years now and I haven't seen him at an event to pick up a copy from him. He's one of the most diligent authors I know when it comes to booking tables so he can put his books in front of new eyeballs. If I haven't seen him behind a table in two years, then I can be relatively sure that I haven't seen anyone.

Now, he's hardly the most prolific of local authors and his books don't have the thickest spines, as he has the opposite mindset of an author like Stephen King, choosing to use one word where one word is needed. That's why he's such a good short story writer and I had a blast with his debut collection, *The Crawlspace*,

far too long ago. Holy crap, has that been out for more than a decade now? I guess it means that I'm a long way overdue reading and reviewing his debut novella, *If It Bleeds*, from 2014.

It runs just shy of a hundred pages, but he has a lot of fun within them, most of it at the expense of an experienced editor in television news, Moses Mayborne, who finds himself returning to his early days as a video journalist and finding that the world has gone batshit insane. And I do mean insane, as he gradually comes to the realisation that the opening line of the back cover blurb isn't kidding at all: "television is killing us".

He works at KAPH-TV, Channel 2 right here in Phoenix, as a crucial back room player in

Commitment2News. His mentor, Alphonso Gonzales, better known as Gonzo, has retired after a couple of decades, due to a sudden blindness. With cuts about to whittle down the Commitment2News work-force, his boss firmly suggests he take a particular promotion and that puts him back on the streets with a camera.

And what he discovers is that, not only are newsworthy stories just as depressing as he remembers, but weird shit is going down: mindless shop employees, arguments in the supermarket, even an altercation at a traffic accident where one driver literally bites off the nose of the other. What really wakes him up to the fact that something is going on is when he reports from a house fire and a cop politely lifts a tarp off a corpse so a passing Dobermann can tear chunks of flesh off its face before wandering back off up the street. That's just not normal, even in Phoenix.

There's a reason behind it all, of course, and Dawson skillfully manouevres us and Moses both towards the eventual explanation, which is dark and pessimistic as it seems likely to be. There's some healthy cynicism here to explore in metaphor, for those who like to dig for meaning, but this works equally as well as a straight read, its horrors right there on the page and of an agreeable level of icky for the more discerning horror hounds.

I'm usually one of those readers who likes to dig for what an author is really talking about and it's not difficult at all to find meaning behind everything that goes down in this fictional Phoenix. However, it isn't the deepest meaning in the world and I think I like this all the more as a straightforward horror story, because it's not merely horrific; it's weirdly horrific. We're not all the way into Bizarro territory but we've definitely crossed the border into a neighbouring surreal state of mind, one that's worthy of a really bad trip. The Dobermanns are the opposite of spirit guides and they make for some wildly memorable scenes.

Of course, I can't talk too much about what goes down in a novella, because the tipping point into the land of spoilers comes early, so this has to remain a shorter review than normal, but that has nothing to do with the quality of the writing. It's telling to me that I recognised my town in this novel, even in a sort of nightmarish mirror image. Dawson is a skilled writer, who can keep things real even while he's making them utterly surreal, and I'll have to remember to thank him in person next time I see him for this trip he took me on. While I buy his new novella, *Death's Dreams*.

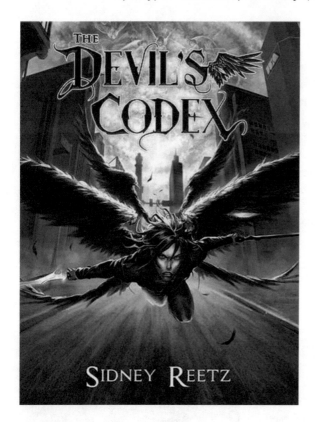

SIDNEY REETZ

THE DEVIL'S CODEX

SAINTS AND SINNERS #1

PUBLISHER:
HELL BAT PUBLICATIONS
PUBLICATION DATE:
DECEMBER 2014

I can't remember how long it's been since I discovered Sidney Reetz at Phoenix Comicon, because she didn't date my copy of *The Devil's Codex* when she signed it, but it was a long time ago, during one of my annual walkabouts through Artist Alley before the vendor hall opens and I have to be back behind my table ready to pimp out my own books. I remember that she was hanging out with the Five Smiling Fish folk, as she often does (they're the first people listed in the thanks list), though she's technically Hell Bat Publications. I still have my plush hell bat and occasionally clip it to my kilt.

Let's just say that it was a long time ago and, like so many books by local authors I've found in similar circumstances, it's languished on my shelves ever since. Yet again, I have to kick myself for not taking it down earlier because it's another peach, a bundle of fun from the outset that only gets better and it's a hard task indeed to put it down to get some sleep at crazy o'clock in the morning.

The basic concept is pretty simple, but also rather thoughtful. What if Lucifer did what he did back in the Fall only because God asked him to do so? After all, it's hard to define good without evil to bounce it off. What if Lucifer has done his duty across the millennia, running Hell and commanding hordes of demons, without ever losing his faith in his father and creator? At what point will he be called home to Heaven, job well done? We often talk about the patience of saints, but what about angels, who might have only fallen in a literal sense?

What prompts action here is the fact that this take on Lucifer is a little worried about his wings. As an impressive early dip into angelology points out, he has six pairs of them and, while they used to be an impressive white, they've been gradually changing to black, to the degree that he only has a few feathers left with white on them. He fears that, when the last one turns completely black, he'll be lost forever like any other demon.

So, he leaves others in charge down there for a while and pops up to rent a room in the appropriately named Lost Port, California, the worst city in the entire United States from any metric you choose, to search for an opportunity to perform some kind of redemptive act. He simply aches to do something good for a change and, if it helps him avoid devolving into a lesser creature in the process, then all the better. Needless to say, he finds plenty of opportunity.

The first thing that springs to mind is that this is a great pitch for an urban fantasy TV show that could be called, I dunno, *Lucifer* or some such. This isn't that *Lucifer*, but it could easily have been in some parallel universe eerily similar to our own in most other respects. The biggest reason why it won't be a TV show is that someone already made something similar enough to prohibit this one ever getting any traction, even if it didn't see airtime until 2016, just over a year after this book was released.

It's still hard not to read *The Devil's Codex* as the first season of a different *Lucifer* though, because of the way that Reetz structures it. She quickly grounds us in her basic idea, so that she can introduce us to the key characters and set all their story arcs into motion

in episode one. Mostly, there's a family who provide him with a home—single mother Ruby Moon, who has some skill with the tarot; her goth teenager Cindy, who goes by Syn; and her utterly endearing three-year-old, Aria, whom Lucifer, going by John Milton (ha), immediately recognises as a much older soul—but others show up over the next few episodes, especially Amanda Rodriguez, the six-and-a-half-foot-tall psychic police detective.

It shouldn't be too surprising to find that other angels join the team as the story runs on, though I'm not going to spoil who or how or when or why. What I will say is there's a serial killer in Lost Port who's taking down high school girls and Lucifer could do a lot worse than enlist the help of these gloriously varied angels as he aims to stop him.

And this leads to a couple of massively important points. One is that glorious variety, because it would have been so easy for Reetz to have conjured up an army of angels, even fallen ones, who all look alike and act in similar ways, because, hey, that's what angels do. She doesn't just successfully resist that urge, she treats the very idea with utter disdain and goes hog wild with her character development. I literally read the introductory chapters for two of these angels with a huge grin on my face. Sure, one of them counts as a form of heresy (no self-respecting Irish pub worth its salt would ever allow a karaoke machine) but it still plays out with such a deft pixielike touch that it's impossible to resist. Best Episode Ever. Well, if we ignore the other one.

Reetz even ends really well. There's a natural ending and there's a supernatural ending, both of which are exactly right and the last page is a great place to wrap with the sure knowledge of more to come. I believe that she's published the second book in the series, *Fallen Saint*, with a novella, *Dealing with Demons*, in between the two, but there will be more. Book three, *Last Martyr*, has been announced and I have no idea if it will mark the end of a trilogy or just another book in a series.

If this review suggests that I simply devoured this book, then you've read right. It runs not too far shy of four hundred pages, but they skipped on by in a mere couple of sessions and I wanted to carry on to the next book, which sadly I haven't bought yet. Maybe if Phoenix Fan Fusion happens in January as it hopes to, I'll get an opportunity then. I like buying my books from the authors; not only because they get signed on the spot.

There is a downside, though, even if it has nothing to do with the writing. It seems like Reetz and her team spellchecked this but didn't proof it properly, because there are a whole slew of words that are real words but the wrong ones for the occasion. There are at least eight instances of "too" instead of "to". Leviathan strums "cords" instead of "chords" and we find Nuriel "dawning" a body not "donning" it. It's hardly on every page, but it's often enough to be frustrating, all the way to the "Epilouge" and the back cover blurb that breaks words between lines without hyphens, so we wonder what "miscon" means. Maybe that's all been fixed with a later edition. I certainly made mistakes with my first books and I still cringe whenever I see the spine to *Velvet Glove Cast in Iron*. Always order the proof copy in print form, folks, even if you miss a self-imposed deadline.

I will now eagerly seek out *Fallen Saint* and watch out for that as one of my monthly Arizona reviews next year. Given how much

fun this was, I'll also prioritise Five Smiling Fish authors, with whom Reetz collaborated on a ghost anthology, *From the Darkest Corner*, with cover art from one of my cover artists, the incomparable Keith Decesare. Did Kira Shay's *Angel's Prophecy* come before Megan E. Vaughn's *The Emerald Door*? I don't think that they're related, outside their shared publisher, but I ought to work through in order.

PS: bonus points for the Within Temptation.

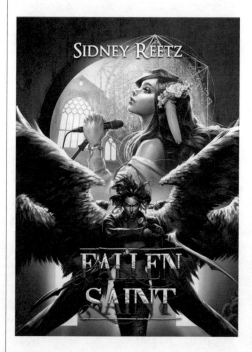

J. A. GIUNTA

THE WARDEN'S LEGACY

PUBLISHER:
BRICK CAVE MEDIA
PUBLICATION DATE:
MAY 2021

In my review of Bruce Davis's *Gold Magic* in June, I noted that I'm getting a little behind with Brick Cave Media publications. I haven't reviewed all that I've read, I haven't read all that I've bought and I haven't bought all that they've published. So, here's one more to help catch up. It's from J. A. Giunta and, if he wasn't the first author they published, he was certainly the most obvious for a while, with his *Ascension Trilogy*. Which I own. And haven't read. Sassinfrassin.

This is a newer book, published early this year, and it's a standalone fantasy novel that's quite unusual in that there's only one human being in it and he doesn't even have a name, though he goes by Crier because he cried a lot as a child, perhaps understandably given that he was being looked after at the time by a dragon and that must have felt rather weird. For quite a while, Crier feels like a MacGuffin, the key to everything, but only a very few characters even know he exists for the longest time.

Frankly, while Crier is massively important to the development of the story, my questions were about Stonefall from moment one. He's the first character we meet and he's also the dragon mentioned above. He's ten years old when we meet him and he's been on his own for five of those, struggling to survive in a unique post-apocalyptic world that may or not be ours. Mankind is gone. The dragons aren't the only species left, but they rule. However, the world around them has been devastated and destroyed and food is scarce.

Most of my questions revolved around what Stonefall is beyond that, because he's clearly different in a number of ways from the other dragons around, who are generally far more stereotypical in that they live up to their beastly representation. Stone is an intelligent and reasoning being and he gets the best of these early, always larger opponents through brain rather than brawn. There's obviously a lot to know about him and we know almost none of it, though, to be fair, neither does he. This novel is as much a voyage of discovery for him as it is for us and we learn at the same time.

The most obvious way Stone distinguishes himself is in what he does when he stumbles on a tree with a passage inside it, leading to an egg surrounded by magic and containing a

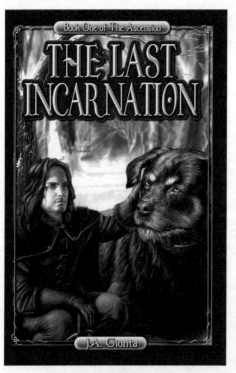

human baby. We get the impression that other dragons would see this as a snack, but Stone finds a way to open the egg and he takes care of the living child who emerges. He also wonders, as we do, at this baby's strange ability to bring life at a touch. Plants spring up around him and the tree starts to return to its expected glory.

To counter this unusual activity, Glim leeches that life away like an energy thief. She's the third major character in our book and, for quite some time, they're the only three who matter. We're kept in the dark about what she is too, though it's clear that she's some sort of fey and she calls herself a Shadow Walker. If we're on Stone's side from moment one, which means that we're inherently on Crier's too, we don't side with Glim as quickly and we're not sure if the others should be associating with her. She could be bad news as easily as she could be good.

It took me a while to appreciate this book, because it builds considerably. It starts out rather simply, a small cast of characters not doing much, and what little they do seems convenient. However, it's very much worth sticking with because our appreciation of the world Giunta that conjures up grows with a succession of revelations. We learn, as Stone learns, what's really going on, not just about him but an increasingly large and varied world. In fact, we re-learn, as Stone re-learns, because it soon becomes clear that he's been lied to all his life, making him an inadvertently unreliable narrator.

And, as we realise that, we ask more and more questions, becoming more and more tied up with the story and the world in which it unfolds, and, as Giunta starts to answer our questions, we appreciate the book all the more. I also appreciate the fast forward button that he presses, because there's no reason for us to watch Crier grow up, even as we note that the book is only two hundred pages long. So Giunta gets these primary characters into a safe space and skips eleven years in seven pages and only then sets up where we're all going to go next.

Because the book is such a revelatory creature, it's difficult to talk about it without leaping headlong into spoiler territory. I'll just say that there are other characters and they belong to many species, not all of them enemies but not all of them friends either, so if I'm giving the impression that this plays it simple and focuses only on three characters, I've hopefully corrected that erroneous implication. We get answers to the vast majority of questions that we pose and it may well be that the ones I had left aren't that important in the grand scheme of things. What's more, the end is very satisfying indeed.

There also aren't a lot of downsides and they're pretty minor. For instance, it's probably not a great idea to call years "turns" in a book about dragons unless it's a deliberate nod to Anne McCaffrey and I don't believe this one is. There's a cutesy character called Notch who has nothing much to do beyond suggest an obvious plush toy if this book should ever be adapted into a Hollywood movie.

There's also the convenience factor which feels like a downside for a while, but I'm not convinced that it actually is. Even though we don't know where the story is going to end up for quite a while, because we don't have information enough to figure that out, there's also a sense of inevitability to it that has an abiding reason to be there that we'll eventually discover. So I think it's an upside that merely feels

as if it could be a downside because of the unusual way in which the book unfolds.

And pretty much everything else I can't talk about because spoilers. Maybe I can sneak in a mention of the first mage scene, because it deserves to be praised as a powerful and impactful setpiece. It's not the only one but it'll stay with me more than the others, I think. For the rest, you'll need to read this yourself. And you should, even though it looks like a younger read than Giunta's other recent books for Brick Cave such as *War Golem* and *Supernal Dawn*, the latter a collaboration with Sharon Skinner. I would say that this one ought to work well as a read for adults as well as young adults.

CHRIS DIETZ

HINTERLAND

PUBLISHER:
HNS PUBLISHING

PUBLICATION DATE:
JANUARY 2019

I've read a lot of books that I enjoyed, some of them a lot; and I've read a lot of books that I didn't enjoy, some of them a lot. However, often the ones that stay with me the longest are the ones that I didn't particularly like but nonetheless appreciated for what they did and what they achieved. That would include a few recent reads like *Everfair* and *Too Like the Lightning*, as well as older Hugo winners like *Lord of Light* and *The Snow Queen*. Early on in this one, I had a feeling that I'd be adding *Hinterland* to that list, because I have to admit that I like what it does a great deal but I can't say that I enjoyed it that much.

What it does and does really well is culture shock. In fact, I'd be hard pressed to come up with another book that does culture shock this well; I'd probably have to go back to J. G. Ballard and Anthony Burgess. I understand culture shock because I'm English but I live in America and we truly are two countries separated by a common language. Even after seventeen years here, I'm still constantly bumping into things that Americans take completely for granted but which make no sense to me at all because I just don't have the same cultural heritage. That sort of culture shock is what most of this book is. And that's often highly confusing.

It's wild from the outset, because it wears its heart on its sleeve, full of wordplay and random slabs of facts, mostly in dialogue, often between a precocious teenage girl named Aurore Arana and Medea, her free spirit of a mother. It's all surreal, jagged, ever moving, often overwhelming and utterly ADHD. I can imagine most readers actually putting this down after the very first chapter to reevaluate whether they're going to continue or not. It's less traditional prose and more a cathartic braindump. And, while it does turn that down a little after that first chapter, it complicates things in other ways and continues to be confusing.

Aurore and her mother are staying at a bed and breakfast on the southern Arizona border with Mexico, when It happens. And It's a big It. Another two kids, Sophie Rose and Tyler Gack, eat some habaneros and manage to rip the fabric of space/time, with this Sophie and Tyler shifting into a parallel universe, while Aurora is watching, and the Sophie and Tyler of that parallel universe shifting over to ours. There are many similarities, whether we're talking about the universes or the kids, but there are big differences as well, major ones. For a start, there are giraffes in this alternate Arizona. And aurochs. And Crots, who are like centaurs who split into two parts.

Differences like those shouldn't be particularly hard to follow and indeed they're not, even as they get bigger and far more obvious as the novel runs on. However, other differences are more of a problem, like the fact that these parallel universe kids speak a variant form of English that I'd call Franglais or Spanglish if it merely chose to add words and phrases from one other language. However, their variant includes not only French and Spanish but German too. These kids are just as culturally confused by our universe as we are to what they expect from theirs, partly due to customs, tech and living creatures varying considerably but also because some of their

words simply have different meanings. Over there, they talk about plastique all the time, but they're not referencing plastic explosive, they're talking about blood or DNA or something I couldn't quite figure out. Because I'm from this side of that rip and they're not.

Had Chris Dietz only gone that far, I think this would have been reasonably simple to decipher, but he has other ideas. Lots of ideas. So, many of the other kids at the bed and breakfast, including Aurore, suddenly wake up to find that they have doubles, because their parallel universe equivalents are right there with them, something that confuses the heck out of their parents and the officials who start to arrive and fail to figure out anything. And, just to layer icing on the cake of confusion, Aurore and her double, who decides to call herself Neo, pretend to be each other, just for kicks and for the intellectual challenge of deceiving everyone else. They're alike in so many ways.

So I like this. I like the ambition on display from a small press author to even attempt something like this. I like how far he took it too, confident in his ability to keep this fundamentally confusing story clear enough that we can follow it without throwing up our hands in despair. I like how Aurore is a highly precocious girl, overly fond of obscure facts and big words. I remember being Aurore and it was fantastic to see a character like that, especially one who's enough of a pixie to just play with the adults around her, especially during such a tough time. And I like that these adults are not the ones who save the day. They are confused from moment one and, while they think they figure some things out as time goes by, they really don't figure out anything. Solving this problem falls to the kids, on both sides of the rip.

But I can't say that I didn't struggle with this. Some of these ideas are fascinating but they make it difficult to follow what's going on. Combining that with wordplay in stream of consciousness can be truly dazzling. And then there are a few bizarre stylistic choices like never spelling out any numbers, even basic ones like two or three. And, of course, doing it all from the very outset makes this quite a challenge. Here's part of page three, to show you what I'm talking about:

"Moods are ways of moving through the world. That's what you tell me. That's what you say all the time. As though you could choose."

"Youth is a world view, my frabjous tortilla chip. You try on all the outfits in all the sizes. And you're an artist too: that makes it worse. Better? My luminous one. Because you can get away with anything. What—am I being harsh? I can't do it— move between worlds the way you do. You know quarks, you know the first 3 minutes. I barely keep up. I have to be professional. Adult. Ha! Numinous one, are you there?" She smirked. "Corona of conflagration, you're an artist!"

"Words are toys. We're just playing. I haven't individuated enough to be objective," the girl murmured.

"Maybe you're feeling an excess of protons this morning? Maybe it's a bit of spoiled cyclotron? I'm kidding. Don't go away. Ma petite microchip. Where are you? Stay with me!"

It isn't quite like that for the whole novel but it's not remotely unrepresentative. And that's the normal bit before the rip happens and characters are shifted or doubled and the languages diversify and the ideas follow suit. It's grounding before it gets truly wild.

So, really, while I liked a lot of what's in *Hinterland* and I appreciated what Chris Dietz was trying to do, just read the paragraph above. If that makes you want to read the book, it's going to knock your socks off, but, if you can't imagine reading more than half a page of that sort of prose, this is absolutely not going to be for you.

Art Town

Chris Dietz

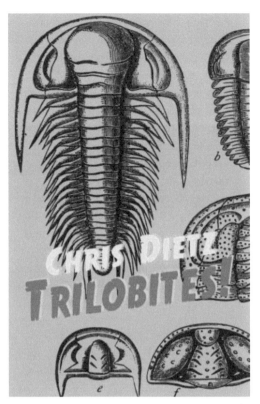

CHRIS DIETZ

TRILOBITES!

PUBLISHER:
HS PUBLISHING

PUBLICATION DATE:
FEBRUARY 2021

So much for chronology. The Nameless Zine received a pair of novels by Chris Dietz as submissions and, as he's an Arizona author, resident in Bisbee, I was happy to give them a go. While they're unrelated standalones, I felt I should tackle *Hinterland* first, given that it saw print first, and then continue on to *Trilobites!* In reality, *Trilobites!* is far more accessible and functions well as a door into his particular style of writing. If you like this, then you may love *Hinterland*, because it does many of the same things but bigger and more and with far more emphasis.

I don't know Dietz's background, beyond the author blurb in these books. He's a writer and a teacher and a birdwatcher and I can see all of those things in his writing. He writes not merely to tell his stories but to have fun with words. His characters are bright, precocious, sometimes modest kids, but believable ones who I'd loved to have known when I was their age. And those characters spend a lot of time outdoors doing the sort of things that kids used to do before technology took over. But he's more than those three things.

In particular, with two of his novels now behind me, I wouldn't be surprised to find that he's also a slam poet and/or a performance artist. His frequent wordplay isn't the traditional sort I'm used to, being an Englishman, not just puns but spoonerisms and malapropisms and their ilk. He goes for jagged stream of consciousness rhyming, like he's a surrealist rapper or, as I said, a slam poet. He likes his homonyms and rhythms and if he can turn them into something quirky and evocative, all the better. He also has a habit of creating characters who also create, the primary ones here being a young writer and a group of important characters who constitute a communal art collective.

That primary character is Ian Scanlan and he's a teenager who's moved to Gary, Indiana with his dad for his work and presumably as part of an ongoing separation. His dad, Ethan, is a teacher and, to be fair, a flaky and bitter pain in the ass. His mum, Taylor, on the other hand is far more stable and interesting, as a geologist mapping aquifers in New Mexico for a mining company. And that's where the trilobites of the title come from. In the cover art, they're the long extinct fossils we know well. In this novel, they live, in a million-year-old underground lake that Taylor and her colleagues discover close to the Texan border. And, considerate mum and corporate risk that she is, she gives Ian one of these trilobites.

I'd say that Ian's a normal kid, but he's a little brighter than the norm, especially so in Gary, Indiana where he's also a fish out of water. For a start, his idiot dad's enrolled him in Catholic school, even though he's an atheist with a fondness for science that he's inherited from his mum. Let's just say that the nuns who run his classes do not appreciate his thoughts on evolution and his not putting God at the heart of each topic they cover. The only friend he makes is an odd one, as she's a nominally Godfearing girl called Bridget who argues with him and apparently hates his guts. But, as is so often the case, that means that they hook up and make a wonderful couple.

Well, not quite. And it isn't just that Ethan arrives home to find his teenage son asleep on his bed with his head on the belly of a sleeping girl he's never seen before. Never mind that

both are fully clothed and nothing untoward happened; you can imagine the shock. It's also that Taylor gradually realises that Hessler, the trilobite she gave to her son, may well be the only male trilobite amongst a population of thousands, if not tens of thousands. His little science project is now a crucial asset of her company, so she wants him back and Ian and Bridget have no intention of letting him get sliced and diced for science.

Being the leads, they naturally figure out a plan and put it into effect and I'm not going to spoil any of it but I should mention two other things. One is that Ian has another couple of friends who factor into this novel in various ways throughout. They're Dan and Tallulah, who pick on each other fondly and viciously, and I have to say that I would be honoured to call either of them friend. Tallulah in particular is a joyous little girl, believably under ten but also believably wise beyond her years. I felt the importance behind every one of her decisions, whether they made sense or not. They certainly did to her.

The other is the other story that unfolds at the same time as the one above, and anyone who looked at the other Chris Dietz that I reviewed at the Nameless Zine, *Hinterland*, will roll their eyes at the likelihood of confusion. Well, yeah, I got confused here for a while too but only for a while and only because of a combination of factors that should probably have been addressed before publication. This story is a fictional story, one that Ian writes throughout the book and which Bridget ends up helping out with.

The main problem is that I didn't realise that it was a fictional story until surprisingly far into the book, even though it's entirely told in italics and even though the fictional story and the real one don't meet in any way other than Ian is in both of them. Had it not been for a couple of crucial things, I would have been fine but whoever proofed the book didn't mention it. One is that the book begins in the fictional story, so we're introduced to Ian not as the character we expect but as a fictional character who simply happens to be based on and invented by the character we expect. The other is that this section ends with an essay that the real Ian wrote for real class but then apparently also included in his fictional story. Hey, it was in italics too, even if they were also bold.

So I didn't recognise the device as a device, even though every other character is different. Instead of a pair of kids that he befriends in Gary, there's a house full of kids that he befriends in Gary, who live over the street without any parental supervision, as they're in a dystopian near future. Instead of going to Catholic school, they do much cooler things, like hack the AIs which run the freight train system so as to be able to sneak into the yards when they're stopped, sneak into specific containers and then sneak out again with stuff they've liberated. And these kids, with their cool names like Romper, Turd and Pop, not to mention the two young hacker girls, Fun and Moon, talk in a rhyming beat poetry, just as ADHD as Aurore's multi-language amalgam in *Hinterland*.

My only problem with this story within a story is that I didn't realise that it was, which issue seems to fall at the feet of the awkwardly conceived and laid out chapter one. Otherwise, I had a blast with it, but I do still wonder why it got such a high page count. There are reasons for it to be there, as insight into what makes Ian tick and as a bonding agent bet-

ween him and Bridget, for a start, but none of the reasons that I conjured up seem to be important enough to warrant that much of it. Maybe I'm missing something. That isn't the hardest thing to do in a Chris Dietz novel.

And, just as I probably came off more positive than I really was in my review of *Hinterland*, I may come off more negative than I really am in my review of *Trilobites!* I liked a lot of the last book but had a lot of problems with it too. I liked more of this one and had fewer problems with it. It's an easier read but it's a similar one in many ways. There's no way that anyone who read the two would mistake them as being by two different authors. Dietz has a very recognisable voice.

The kids are the important characters in both books and they share a slew of attributes that the author obviously appreciates. The adults were utterly useless in *Hinterland* and some in this book are utterly useless too, but they're given reasons beyond simply being adults, making this a far more mature work: Ethan is bitter about the collapse of his marriage and he's moving slowly into crazy town, while Bridget's mum is a religious nut. Other adults, though, are capable if flawed human beings, like Ian's mum, along with the dedicated Officer Mahoney and a talented PI by the name of Hakeem Arafat. Both books are road movies and coming of age stories with the girls generally smarter than the boys.

Dietz only has one further novel in print, namely *Art Town*, published later in 2021, after *Trilobites!* What little I can see about it suggests that it's likely to unfold in a similar way to the two I've read, which bodes well, because I like Dietz's unique voice and, on the basis of only two books, is improving at getting it across. Maybe I'll track it down and give it a shot too.

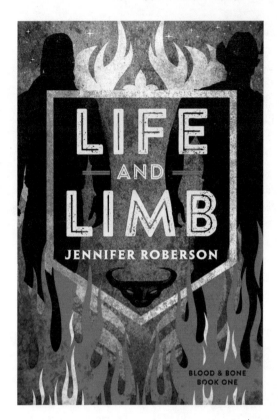

JENNIFER ROBERSON

LIFE AND LIMB

BLOOD AND BONE #1

PUBLISHER:
DAW BOOKS

PUBLICATION DATE:
NOVEMBER 2019

This one has sat on my TBR shelf for longer than it should have done, but I pulled it out to get signed at TusCon and felt it should also become my Arizona review this month. I'm not quite sure why I didn't dive into it sooner but part of it may be that Roberson is a thoroughly established and acclaimed writer of fantasy who's writing outside her usual genre. Did I really think that she was jumping on the urban fantasy bandwagon twenty years too late? Maybe subconsciously I did.

But now I'm happy I dived in. It took me a while to warm to this book but I did warm to it and I'm eager to see where Roberson takes the series, which could run on for a long time, even longer than the seven *Tiger and Del* books or the eight in the *Chronicles of the Cheysuli*. The

biggest problem I had with this one was that it ended, because it serves emphatically as a beginning but not seemingly a complete one.

If what I'm imagining the series to be feels a lot like a TV show (and *Supernatural* is so clear a comparison that it's actually referenced in the text), this first novel feels very much like the first half of a feature length pilot. Hang about for the second half after the break... except that the break turns out to be two years long because *Sinners and Saints* wasn't released until this year. What's odd is that, while it seems like a clearly bad thing to cut off the story like that, I'm not convinced that it really is.

And that's the same sort of thinking that meant that I had to warm to this. It felt off a lot, but when I thought about why it felt off, the logic seemed to be not only fair but refreshing. So I did what I rarely do and checked out what other reviewers have said about this. What I found that's really interesting to me is that most of the things that people didn't like are the things that I did, at least once I thought about them.

The most obvious example is the fact that the spur for the story is jarring to its heroes and I'm struggling to remember the last time I read that in urban fantasy. Every take on the genre seems to reveal a hidden world to the protagonist who responds with an immediate acceptance, like an invisible shrug, and on we go as if the hidden world was never hidden. That doesn't happen here and, while it initially seemed annoying, it was the single aspect that I ended up appreciating the most.

The protagonists are Gabriel Harlan and Remiel McCue, a pair of young men who were apparently born at almost exactly the same date and time, which I'm sure is notably important for reasons that we don't know yet. Otherwise, they're different in most regards, Gabe being a biker from Portland who's fresh out of prison and Remi being a cowboy from Texas who loves country music. But they both have a Granddaddy, the same Granddaddy, who isn't actually related to either of them, and he's who kicks this off.

He's an agent of Heaven, he explains to them at their first meeting, in a roadhouse in Flagstaff, Arizona. They're not angels but they do have Heavenly stuff in them and it's time for them to know that because they'll have to work together as a pair to use it to thwart the emergence of Satan and an otherwise imminent Apocalypse. In particular, they'll need to hunt demons, who will manifest as any number of mythological beasts or creatures, starting with a couple of ghosts.

Just imagine yourself in that situation. You trust your Granddaddy who's been there for you all your life, but he introduces you to a complete stranger and springs all that on you. He gives you a ring and explains, very vaguely, that you've been training your whole life, without you knowing it, to save the world from the forces of evil. And you're not even religious. Yeah, it's going to sound completely batshit insane and I just don't buy into a quick acceptance. Even when weird shit goes down, that doesn't mean that this half-explanation covers everything.

And so Gabe and Remi struggle, not just initially but through the entire book, with an immense change in their life. So they successfully kill a demon by shooting the ghost it occupied with a holy weapon. What does that mean for their new reality? What else is real? What are the rules? What are the boundaries? What's still batshit insane even in this new reality? Who knows? Who can know? How wild is this going to get? I'd have so many questions in this situation and that makes me appreciate why Gabe and Remi feel so utterly refreshing when they feel so lost.

After all, the initial reaction to the revelation that God and Satan are apparently real ought to be that the other stuff that we've read about in the Bible is real too. That ought to be the new framework to accept, right? And that includes the obscure stuff, because a Grigori soon shows up to warn them that Granddaddy has an agenda that he's hiding. Grigoris are watchers, fallen angels who tend to sire Nephilim with human women. Of course, this Grigori is female and Asian just to mess with that assumption.

But then we meet the Morrigan, as in the Morrigan of Celtic legend, goddess of battle, along with her sisters, who appear here as a wolfhound and a crow. Now, the Morrigan is hardly traditional, because she now has a red Mohawk and wicked tattoos that move and she drives an expanding RV because she occupies the Q role we know from *James Bond* movies, but the point is that she's not at all Christian. She's from Celtic mythology, so us opening up to accept a Christian framework just isn't enough. So what else?

How about Aganju, the bartender at the Zoo Club in Flagstaff? He's an Igbo orishi, so from Nigeria, and he's a god of volcanoes. Apparently there are six hundred of those here in Arizona, which blew my mind, and he sings them into life. That's just about as far from Christianity as it gets. Roberson brings in a whole slew of mythologies and religions and cultures to populate this novel with characters. And the demons that have found their way into our world are occupying creatures of folklore, which now exist because they believe them so.

Needless to say, Gabe and Remi are wildly unprepared for any of this and they're not remotely ready to identify domiciles and hunt surrogates and whatever else they are now tasked with doing without having a clue what any of these things are, let alone a suggestion of what they do and how they do it, not to even approach how to stop it. In that context, it seems like a duh that they're frustrated and always questioning, but it really is something that I've not seen in urban fantasy before.

Of course, given that we learn about this stuff as they learn about it, which is usually at the most critical and dangerous moments, there's so much that we don't know yet. We're going to learn more in the next book, I'm sure, but, the way we're going, we'll be still learning crucial information ten books in, because the scope is so vast and the possibilities are so varied that it's hard to put a boundary around it to even figure out what questions to ask. We're not even close.

And, of course, this is firmly an origin story, or at least the beginning of one, with not a lot of room for actual plot. We're facing Armageddon and somehow these two guys are the potential solution: that's the plot. This book is about introducing us to the basic idea, the protagonists we'll follow and the supporting characters who will help or stir things up, as well as a little doubt cast on what we can believe. Is Granddaddy telling the whole truth and nothing but the truth or is he an unreliable teacher with his own agenda that he's keeping secret from everyone, including us? We just don't know.

And, in a genre where most things tend to be explained quickly and accepted even quicker, I would call this a breath of fresh air. Now, let's get into a real story set within this wild framework with *Sinners and Saints*. I need to go buy that one.

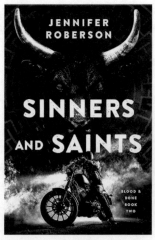

DANI HOOTS

A WORLD OF VAMPIRES VOLUME 1

A WORLD OF VAMPIRES #1

PUBLISHER:
CREATESPACE

PUBLICATION DATE:
DECEMBER 2014

I'm not entirely sure when I picked up this book and its first sequel from the author at a convention. I'm pretty sure it was one of the Phoenix Comicon Fan Fests in Glendale, as I vaguely remember her table being somewhere in the University of Phoenix Stadium, on that unforgiving concrete floor, so that means 2014 or 2015.

At that point, she'd written nine novellas in this series, plus a trilogy of others called *A Falling Starr*. Since then, it looks like she's written a lot more, mostly YA novellas in an array of series and genres: a sci-fi trilogy called *Sanshlian*, the *Wonderland* quartet and *City of Kaus*, an LGBTQ+ sci-fi western duology. At novel length, there's an urban fantasy quartet called *Daughters of Hades*, and there's more at a

shorter length. She has clearly kept herself very busy indeed.

And, while this does feel like early work, it's also enjoyable stuff that shows a heck of a lot of promise and I'm not surprised that she's been able to build on this with so much more work. It was the cover art by Daniel Somerville that grabbed me first, painted in dark watercolours, and the concept finalised the deal as it's right up my alley. This first volume is a collection of the first four stories in the series, each titled for and revolving around a breed of vampire that is not the one you expect, even with one story set in Romania.

The four are listed on the back cover, each accompanied by a brief synopsis, and it was telling that I didn't recognise all of them. As a

Brit, I knew about the baobhan sith (and that it's pronounced banshee) and the strigoi come up a lot. As a big fan of hopping vampires in Asian cinema, I was ecstatic to see a jiangshi included, but I didn't recognise a hooh-strah-dooh. What I found is that it's a peculiarly Native American form of vampire, tied here to a single tribe, the Wyandot.

That's an odd synchronicity for me, given that my genealogical work on the family that I married into show that my kids have Wyandot ancestry eleven generations back, with Jane Sandusky the daughter of Chief Steven Sandusky and "Wyandot Maiden". I chose to say that here because there's another odd synchronicity in play too. While I don't believe I've seen Dani Hoots's name since I bought these two books from her maybe seven or eight years ago, but suddenly it's showing up everywhere. That's a good thing, right?

Hooh-Strah-Dooh comes first and it sets the template in place, the worst thing about the book being that the first three novellas have a

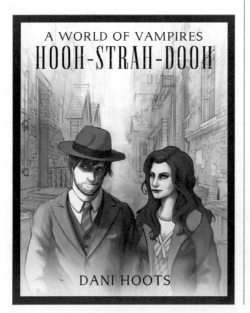

very similar sweep, even though they're told in different ways otherwise. Each unfolds in the first person and is recounted by a vampire who has lived until the present day and is kind of pissed at how modern media presents vampires as inherently romantic creatures. Each of these vampires was turned against their will and deeply wants to cease to be. That's a lot of consistent pessimism, so it's refreshing when the fourth story changes that up completely.

The other trend is that each story becomes shorter, to the degree that the first surely has to be a novella but the last only a short story and the two in between of a length I couldn't be sure is a novella or a novelette. That's fine, of course, but the presentation of stories in an order where they get progressively less substantial is a surprising one and not a choice I'd have made, especially as these stories could be easily read in any order. I assume that they're chronological by original release.

Given that some of that is negative, I'll get the rest out of the way quickly. The prose is initially clumsy, though I got quickly sucked into the story anyway, by which point it did pick up. I've read a lot worse, from professional authors, but it's clear that Dani Hoots was learning her trade and I'm not going to hold a few clumsy paragraphs, or indeed a few badly proofed typos, against her. This stands on her imagination and her idea, and both are good.

The rest is positive. I liked the variety in the vampire mythologies, even if three ended up in a similar mindset; the Wyandot concept of the vampire was something new to me and I appreciated that a great deal. I also liked the variety of times and places in which these stories were set. *Hooh-Strah-Dooh* begins in Boston in 1931 and is centered around an Irish

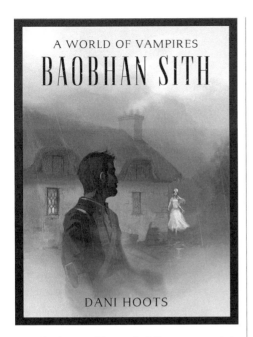

gang leader. *Baobhan Sith* follows an English army captain heading south with the remnants of his company after Culloden. *Strigoi* is set in 16th-century Romania and *Jiangshi* in San Francisco during the California Gold Rush.

And, even if I was turned off by the consistency in opinion of these vampires, I liked the variety in tones that got them to that point. *Hooh-Strah-Dooh* is emphatically gothic in nature, a *Beauty and the Beast*-esque romance with a benefactor who takes a servant who he eventually frees, only to discover that she won't leave. The guilt is hard and strong in this one, across characters, and that leads to tragic bitterness. *Baobhan Sith* has a very different tragedy and the focus is on responsibility rather than guilt. In *Strigoi*, everything feeds off power, almost the entire story under a hypnotic spell that was woven by a seductive violin. *Jiangshi* returns to guilt, but explores it in a different fashion, driven by betrayal.

I enjoyed this a great deal and fully plan to

follow up with book two. That one takes an even deeper dive into the realm of vampire lore across the world, its four stories also given titles for their respective vampires, this time more obscure names: *Asanbosam, Lilith, Peuchen* and *Aufhocker*. Excepting *Lilith*, I have no idea what those are and I'm eager to find out. And yes, if you're paying attention, you'll remember that I said that there were nine original novellas, meaning that there's one more not currently swept up into a collection, and that's *Soucouyant*, another new one on me.

I'm hoping to see Dani Hoots at another convention at some point, so I can purchase her other books. While YA is hardly my go-to reading level, I'm intrigued by a few series with her name on them and the rest of them ought to work well for either my better half or my eldest granddaughter. I want to know more about what her imagination conjures up and I want to see her mature as a writer.

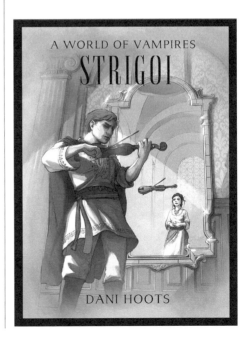

JAMES SABATA

THE CASSOWARY

PUBLISHER:
CREATESPACE

PUBLICATION DATE:
NOVEMBER 2020

This month's Arizona author for me is the author and podcaster James Sabata, for a few reasons. One is that I've planned to review more horror here at the Nameless Zine—hey, it's a perfectly valid genre within the wider one of fantastic fiction. Another is that I swapped a copy of one of my books for *The Cassowary* at TusCon 48 as James and I shared a signing table. And a notable third is that the two words that kick off the novel constitute the name of my eldest son, who quickly thereafter becomes an ex-son, the first victim of the titular monster bird. This particular cassowary mangles, maims and murders a varitey of real people within the pages of this book, a whole slew of whom I know personally or, at least, recognise. That's fun.

It's worth mentioning that I've been a true sucker for creature horror since I discovered it in the eighties, as those of you reading my Guy N. Smith runthrough reviews will have seen already. Over the many decades since, horror authors have continued to work their way through the animal kingdom, tracking down a variety of new creatures yet to be given their own rampages and I have to admit to shock that not one of the many horror novelists out there had enlisted the cassowary until now. After all, we all know that big birds are often vicious, even if we've never been chased by a goose or a swan, and the southern cassowary, the most common variety of the species, is both the third tallest and the second heaviest living bird on the planet. It deserves its own moment in the creature horror spotlight.

My son is an old man here, which makes me

wonder all the more about the grey in my beard, and he's worked at the Toscano Wildlife Preserve here in Phoenix for a quarter of a century. In that time, he's trained legions of keepers and doted on generations of animals. Cassie, the zoo's cassowary, used to sit in his lap when she was young. Of course, she's not young any more and, what's more, she's not at all herself. As the tagline has it: "The world's most dangerous bird just got an upgrade". Something has happened to Cassie, something that's generating bright pink light in her eyes and prompting her to go batshit crazy on a doting keeper like Michael Flanders. Oh well, she's got to start somewhere, right? We'll miss you, dude.

If there's a plot here, it's this. Cassie, previously a popular exhibit at the zoo, is now a deadly fugitive who's wreaking havoc across town, leaving an increasingly bloody trail in her wake and a burgeoning news story to panic the local populace. The zoo has to get her back or, at least, to stop her before the death count grows any larger, so it sends out security guard Jerome McClintock and animal handler Kaitlyn Lenhart to get the job done. Of course, that's much easier said than done, because Cassie is not merely gone, she's also changed, growing in size and threat with each kill for reasons we don't know but surely have to be supernatural. I may not know much about cassowaries but I'm pretty sure they don't emanate pink light from their eyes like laser beams. Unless they're leading a pride parade.

The chapters generally alternate between Jerome and Kaitlyn doing what they can, along with some other people searching for Cassie for their own purposes, and the cassowary carving her way through a substantial cast of freshly introduced and quite clearly disposable characters. There's really not too much else here, which is both a positive and negative. Those looking for depth will find this a shallow read, without much at all in the way of character development or plot. However, anyone looking for a novel where a cassowary kicks ass and takes names, with surprising speed and the deadly 5" middle claws on its feet, is going to get exactly that. *The Cassowary* delivers exactly what it promises. It merely doesn't do a heck of a lot else. OK, we learn why the supernatural, but that's not much of a surprise.

What's perhaps most surprising about this book is that it was written as part of a charity series with profits going to protect the bloodthirsty creatures in their titles. Inspired by a headline shared by a group of horror authors on Twitter, Alan Baxter quickly wrote

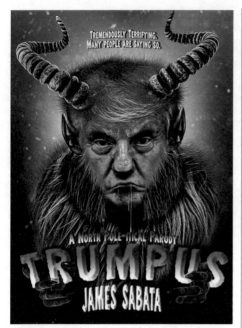

given that name, clearly those running the Toscano Wildlife Preserve should have hired them to track down Cassie, but that would have left this novel a short story, so we should be thankful that they went with Jerome and Kaitlyn.

Now, having got the author's signature on my copy of *The Cassowary*, I clearly need to add that of my son and everyone else I know here in Phoenix who Sabata tuckerised here for posterity. Hey Brian! And John! And AJ! And...

a horror novel starring a kangaroo, *The Roo*. Stephanie Rabig followed up with *Playing Possum*, which I simply have to seek out, and Sean Seebach contributed *The Buck Stops Here*. Forgetting that each author wrote about an animal supposedly native to his or her home locality, Sabata successfully pitched *The Cassowary*, even though the bird is completely not native to Arizona.

Of course, nobody cares about that, especially as Sabata never pretends that it is. Cassie's in the zoo here and she's deadly and she escapes after her mysterious upgrade and that's all we care about. We can sit back and bathe in the blood she sprays over every other chapter, secure in the knowledge that there will be another one and another and... And, having revelled in Cassie's carnival of carnage, we can be immensely happy that the profits will go to the Cassowary Recovery Team, a group of groups working together to protect both cassowaries and their habitats. Of course,

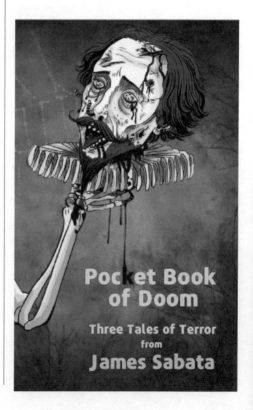

JEFF MARIOTTE

THE SLAB

PUBLISHER:
IDW PUBLISHING
PUBLICATION DATE:
OCTOBER 2003

Jeff Mariotte may not have lived in Arizona when he wrote *The Slab*, residing in San Diego at the time as a co-owner of the Mysterious Galaxy bookshop, but he lives here now and he's a mainstay of the local author community. I've read a few of Jeff's dark thrillers in the past, like *Cold Black Hearts* and *River Runs Red*, but only one recently enough to review it at the Nameless Zine, so it's about time I tackled another and I've long admired this cover.

It's an interesting one because of how it goes about its business. It's a novel but it doesn't play like one. As a broad story, the big picture that's behind everything is surprisingly simple, unfocused until late and wrapped up pretty quickly without a firm explanation of the how behind the much clearer why. However, as negative as that sounds, none of it

matters, because that grand sweep is timeless and omnipresent, the eternal battle between good and evil, and this uses it more as the backdrop to a set of smaller stories than as the be-all and end-all.

As the back cover blurb tells us, there are three separate characters with initially separate stories which gradually interweave as the book runs on until they find that they're really a trio of threads to a bigger story. All of that's true, but mostly just a tease. It doesn't tell us which three characters, for a start, so we're kept on the hop figuring out which they are, while Mariotte introduces us to a massive ensemble cast. Also, it doesn't easily translate to three stories taking up a third of the book each; it's more like a couple of novellas and a host of short stories that make up a third.

The first of the three primary characters is obvious, because the opening part of the book is given his name, even though it's far from all about him. He's Kenneth Butler and he's a sheriff out in the wilds of eastern California, a good man but a troubled one. He lost his wife in a tragic accident and crawled into a bottle, but he eventually crawled out again and found himself a job with jurisdiction over the Slab, a collection of misfits and ne'er-do-wells who have opted out of society for reasons of their own and who come together in a ramshackle RV community in between the Chocolate Mountains and the Salton Sea. However, the Slab is as much a character as anyone else here.

We know the Slab is important because it's the title of the book and a frequent location for events; but we don't know why and we won't for most of the novel. It's a fantastic backdrop, an utterly unique community that really exists. Slab City's website is down right now and Jeff's own photos of it have vanished after his recent website revamp, but a quick search on Google Images is enough to tell me that I've seen video and photos of this place before, especially of its abundant art. Mariotte introduces us to a host of residents and I wonder how many of them were inspired by real people. Surely not all, given how troubled some of them get. At least I hope so.

We also don't know why Sheriff Butler is important but we know he is, because he feels the magic. It's a strange feeling, one that pops up now and again in his life at odd moments, always heralded by the taste of copper in his mouth. The first time for him was during the Vietnam War, when he was down inside an enemy tunnel system and he was kept safe and guided out by a talking snake, and it's not left him ever since, not really. I appreciated this take on magic. It's not something that Butler can conjure up at will to do his bidding. It comes when it comes and it always manifests in some new strange way, then leaves again. It's elusive and indefinable and, while it seems to be a positive thing, that's up for debate.

We recognise the second of the primary characters, as she feels the magic too. She's a veteran too, but a younger one who served in Iraq, coming home wounded but alive after a magic incident in which she was able to mysteriously keep a convoy safe in a minefield. She's Penny Rice and the third part is named for her. While Sheriff Butler is upholding the law, she's breaking it but for what she believes is a very important reason. We first meet her as she sneaks onto the military test site not far from the Slab to make rock art messages like "No More Bombs".

I'm not going to name the third character, as who it is doesn't really become clear until very late. Initially I thought it was real estate mogul Carter Haynes, who's bought the Slab and the land around it to develop into almost the precise opposite of Slab City: a community of luxury residences. He's the first character we meet and he's important to the story, but he's not the third of the primaries any more than Lucy Alvarez is and she feels as close to a lead as anyone does.

That's because the most obviously developing story in the book is the Dove Hunt, an annual event for a group of men, gathered together by Kerry, a special forces veteran, who kidnap a woman, who tends to be brown-skinned and dark-haired, off the streets to be the Dove in their take on the Most Dangerous Game. There are thirteen graves in the desert and we can't help but wonder if the human skull found in the firepit at the Slab and handed over to Sheriff Butler is from one of them. Lucy proves to be a tougher Dove than they've hunted before and she doesn't merely survive. As the Sheriff investigates the skull and searches for Lucy, we wonder if she's just part of his story, but the weaving of threads runs far deeper than that.

Eventually, all these stories, plus others too, start to converge and transform into parts of something more. There's also another note that runs through this novel, which is 9/11. It isn't part of the story, having happened a week or two before anything we read, but it flavours many stories here, as Mariotte wrote this in the aftermath of that terrorist act and it weighs on the minds not only of the various military veterans in the story, or indeed those still active, but plenty of the other characters too, as they're Americans too. After all, the attacks weren't just against buildings but the American way of life and it was very hard for Americans not to take that personally.

I liked this novel a lot, more than the other Mariottes that I've read, even though they were more traditional. This one feels less like a novel and more like an energizing, fascinating and traumatic trip away from everything. It plays like immersion in an escape, the result of which is partly freedom and partly responsibility. There are many reasons to opt out of everything and live on the Slab and it's a fantastic sanctuary from some angles, but freedom comes with a price and the Slab isn't a cure all. It's a tough life living in the middle of a blazing desert without electricity and running water or most of the other comforts of life that the rest of us take for granted.

And that's what this book becomes. It's a rumination on 9/11, knowing that it's going to change the country in fundamental ways but wondering about how that'll play out. It's also a look at society, a look at what it means and how it works, but done by looking at people who have chosen to opt out of it—some the responsibilities, some the rules, some just the grind, some the morality, some the reality—only, of course, to create their own rules and morality and responsibilities.

There are a lot of points where characters in this book come to realisations, not the overt lightbulb moments that chapters are designed around but more subtle ones where characters realise that their vision of the world wasn't quite right. There's much growth here and we can't help but read *The Slab*, with all its death and madness and immorality, as being fundamentally about hope. This was a notably dark time and Mariotte both acknowledges that and suggests that we could, if only we can come together, defeat the darkness. I should have read this sooner.

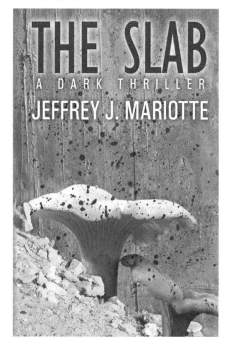

MONA VENTRESS

ANOINTED BY ANUBIS

LOVER OF MYTHIC PROPORTIONS #1

PUBLISHER:
WORDSMITH INDUSTRIES

PUBLICATION DATE:
FEBRUARY 2022

I've stepped outside my comfort zone a few times this month, reading books that don't sit in genres I'm known for reading. However, if I thoroughly enjoyed the alternate black history of *The Conductors* and preferred the romantic suspense in *Fatal Code* to its technological thrills, why not dive into some smut for this month's Arizona author?

Officially, of course, this is erotica/fantasy/adventure, but that's only a fancy way to describe smut. We shouldn't fool ourselves on that front, just as we shouldn't fool ourselves in other ways, like assuming that smut is what people write when they can't write. That's unfair and this is a great example of that, because, beyond being smut, it's well-written and not at all what you're conjuring up. For a start, while the pages almost drip with juices

simply aching to be put to good use, there's a lot less actual sex here than I was expecting.

I've met Mona Ventress at a few previous events before, but I bought *Anointed by Anubis* from her this year at Wild Wild West Steampunk Convention. It's the first in an ambitious series of what must strictly be called novellas, called *Lover of Mythic Proportions*, a delightful play on words, given that the focus is that our heroine, Delilah Hansen, is going to spend that series getting it on with a complete alphabet of gods and other mythological mainstays. No prizes for guessing who's first in line, as it were. *Buzzed on Bacchus* is next and then it's *Capturing Centaurs*. I don't know that Zeus will be last in line, but it's a safe bet, given that he got it on with pretty much anyone and anything on the planet, if you read far enough into Greek mythology.

Everything I write here ends up sounding like an intended double entendre and I simply don't have time enough to avoid all of them, so I guess I'll throw caution to the wind and point out that I had a absolute blast (oh dear) with *Anointed with Anubis*, even though men in general are hardly seen positively here at all. In fact, the one with the largest part (see what I mean) doesn't even show up, except in magical flashbacks, because it's Delilah's ex, Jason, who unfortunately assumed, after she confessed certain rougher fantasies to him, that it was his job to effectively rape her without the benefit of a safe word. "The more you cry, the more I'm going to hurt you," does not bode well for a loving relationship and that's why he's an ex.

That's also why Delilah has sworn off men entirely for a few years. After all, as the back cover blurb so memorably has it, "Why even take a risk on someone when vibrators exist?" The catch is that electronic help only goes so far for someone who's actually named her lady parts, which also talk to her, almost constantly, about bringing home something less reliant on batteries and more attached to a human being for her to play with. By now, Delilah is getting pretty close to the point where she can't function as a freelance accountant any more without VJ, her pleading privates, promptly stealing her attention away to satisfy its (her?) own needs.

Fortunately, there's a solution, as she soon discovers when Hermes, the messenger of the gods, appears in her apartment mid-session. He's not there to answer VJ's call, he's there to deliver an invitation and that he just about manages to do so without the early chapters turning into the book's first sack session is a

good indicator of what we can expect here and what we can't. Yes, there are sex scenes, albeit fewer in number than we might expect, but there's also a lot of humour, not entirely situational, and an actual honest-to-goodness story. Sure, the premise is pretty straightforward—Hermes's message is to suggest that she "end her self-imposed celibacy by getting it on with the gods". It's right there in the blurb on the back cover, but it's explained in more appropriate detail within the text.

In many ways, this first volume doesn't exist merely to knock off the first encounter, though it does that; it serves to introduce the internal logic of the series and set everything in motion. It's an origin story for our lover of mythic proportions, which has more meanings than you initially thought. For a start, it's a reference not only to the legendary appendages of legendary beings but to Delilah herself, who freely admits to not being skinny or beautiful or charming. Hermes begs to disagree, suggesting that her "body type was considered the archetype of perfection" in his time.

What's more, joining this sex club literally of the gods isn't as simple as just saying yes. Delilah must die and be resurrected before she can take part and, when it comes to the gods, everything is ritual. That's why Anubis is first in line. Wearing the metaphorical hat of the Egyptian god of the dead, he can guide her through all those rituals with all the required gravitas. Then he can switch hats to a god whose name begins with A and attempt to acquiesce the almost apoplectic VJ, who's been waiting far too long, thank you very much.

I'm not a regular reader of smut, but I've read enough during research into authors who have churned out hundreds of thousands of words of the stuff to know that it gets old very quickly. There are only so many ways to talk about how X goes into Y, after all. What matters in erotica isn't that, or isn't only that. To be more accurate, it's building a story in which that happens, cast with characters who we want to be doing that, while we watch. I thought I might enjoy this book, given its wild premise and what the author told me about it when we chatted in Tucson. However, I didn't think I'd enjoy it as much as I ended up doing.

Sure, it's a hundred and twenty pages or so of panting anticipation, followed by the payoff that you're expecting, which is entirely appropriate, but it's a lot more than that too. It's also a novella that's funny and evocative and, dare I say it, a little educational. I may not be aching for the sequel quite as much as VJ, who is clearly struggling in vain to keep her fluids in check, but I'll certainly pick up a copy of *Buzzed on Bacchus* when I see the author at another event.

TOM LEVEEN

SICK

PUBLISHER:
AMULET BOOKS
PUBLICATION DATE:
OCTOBER 2013

Tom Leveen is a pristine example of why I'm reviewing an Arizona author every month at the Nameless Zine. I've met him a number of times, he's a nice guy and he gives good panel. My better half was even in one of his book promo videos, though not for this one. I've bought a few books from him over quite a few years that he's kindly signed for me, and I haven't read any of them. So, it's clearly about time that I fixed that and this YA zombie novel is the one I pulled off the shelf. I read it over a couple of train journeys in the UK in April and, while I had to refresh myself on the details, the feel of it all stayed with me.

The tagline, almost inevitably, is *The Breakfast Club* meets *The Walking Dead* and, for once, that's an almost appropriate description. It doesn't take much to find flaws with the first half of that, but it's not entirely out of place. Our protagonists are a disparate group of ne'-er-do-well schoolkids who aren't bad enough to strip our sympathy from them, even our narrator, Brian, who we quickly learn dumped Laura, his girlfriend of a year and a half as the medication she's on to control her emotions because of a panic disorder suppresses everything else too, including, so it's hinted, her libido. So Brian's a selfish asshole of a teenager because he's not getting much, but perhaps, a believable one. To be fair, that decision does haunt him throughout this novel as the apocalypse shows up.

Brian and his friends Chad and Jack are supposed to be at school at this point, but they're not because they decided to skip a few classes to eat microwaved pizza over at Chad's place. That means that they miss a few key isolated incidents, like a fight in the gym that led to someone's finger being bitten off, but they're inevitably let in on the apocalypse. They see their friend Hollis, who'd called out seriously sick, because his seven-year-old kid brother Kyle bit him that morning. His mum's sicker still. The streets are emptied and the news reporters are trying to figure out what's going on at Phoenix Memorial Hospital. The CDC is apparently in town. And Brian's mum is an investigator at the county medical examiner's office who calls to let him know that she's been called out to a small town called Arroyo where weird things are happening.

Eventually, and it doesn't take too long to get through four or five skipped classes, they head back over to Phoenix Metro High School,

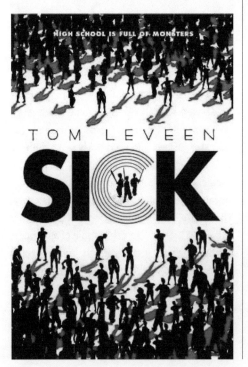

driven by a few things. For one, they don't want to miss seventh period theatre because Mrs. Golab would be pissed and it's an easy blow-off class for them. For another, most of the school is going to the pep rally instead, crucially including Laura and her best friend Kenzie, who's also Brian's sister. Brian may be an asshole but he wants to protect Laura, not only because of the guilt wracking him after dumping her, and he wants to protect Kenzie too, whom he won't ever forget nearly died seven years ago. And the girls are messaging him that there's a huge fight at the pep rally.

Where we go from here is mostly as you'll expect but I don't think it's fair to say that you can write the rest yourself. Tom Leveen writes smooth prose that skims along effortlessly, almost like he could teach classes on writing YA—he can and he does—but he's not above flouting our expectations whenever he feels an abiding need. No, I'm not going to spoil the book, but I will say that not everyone you'll take for granted will survive actually does. It's testament to Leveen's skills as an author that, whenever a whoa! moment is sprung on us, we feel the emotions that we're supposed to, even if we're fifty-something grandparents.

I will mention a few things that perhaps I shouldn't though. One is that Laura is one of the characters to survive. Is that a spoiler? Only kinda sorta, because it's so clear from her condition that she absolutely has to be a quick and easy victim that she just as clearly isn't going to be and I think everyone reading this book surely has to make that same assumption. The school is effectively under lockdown, with steel fences around the campus that have spikes on the top. Zombies, or whatever they are, are inside the grounds and they are strong and fast and eager to indulge in a smörgåsbord of tasty morsels trying to hide from them. If Laura died, I don't think there's a single reader who would forgive the author for that.

Another is that, while the core clique we follow does include some pretty fit and tough people, like Chad who is aching to sign up for the Marines and Cammy who leads the cheerleader squad, the heroes of the day are really the theatre department and, by that, I mean the students who work it. They spend their time building things and taking things down and meeting every need, so it's maybe not too surprising that they may be best equipped to combat a zombie infestation. However, it's not what we expect from a YA novel. Theatre isn't a cool class, right? Those dudes are nerds and cool kids are supposed to laugh and pick on them. I've seen American high school movies.

So kudos to Tom Leveen for creating believably damaged characters like Brian, Kenzie and Laura, none of whom feel like typical YA characters but none of whom feel unbelievable either. And kudos to him for making the stage nerds the heroes. In fact, let's throw some more kudos at him for making this quite a gorefest for a YA novel. There are definitely some edgy scenes here but they never really transcend the undefined (or maybe defined) boundaries between YA and adult fiction. No adult will read this and feel that it's a horror novel. It's always a YA horror novel and those two letters are pretty important.

There are things that I won't give him kudos for though. Some of the little subplots he sets into motion are not resolved and it's not due to the likelihood of a sequel. They just fall by the wayside, perhaps understandably for a zombie apocalypse but not for a crafted novel. There are some plot holes that I noticed, most of them to do with the capabilities that he

gives these zombies and what we realise when we try to view the school rather than a single character. Realistically, Leveen believably sets up everyone to die, quickly and efficiently, but then has to conjure up ways for some of them to get out and, while we enjoy how he does that, we don't ever fully buy into them.

Now, those aren't big complaints and they don't nullify the success that this book is but, if I was Brian's theatre teacher and forced to rate this, I'd knock off some marks. I'd still recommend this book to teenagers though, and even to older audiences who might not be as drawn to YA generally. It also makes me interested in reading some of his other YA books that I've bought over the years that looked, well, a bit angsty. This is higher rated at Goodreads than *Manicpixiedreamgirl*, but not *Random*, *Zero* or *Party*. That bodes well.

ETHAN MOE

RIDER

PUBLISHER:
STRANGE ANGEL PRESS
PUBLICATION DATE:
APRIL 2013

I can't remember at which convention I bought this book from its author, but it had to be a convention because Ethan Moe is a long time member of Phoenix fandom, who even chaired a LepreCon in 2009, albeit a relaxacon during a very busy year for events. It's his first novel and, while the bio at the back suggests that a couple more were coming soon in 2013, including a sequel to this book, they don't seem to have arrived yet. And that's a shame, because I enjoyed this. While it's not a particularly deep novel at two hundred pages, it's an enjoyable one that introduces an interesting mythology.

Initially, it appears to be a horror novel, because page one is horrific indeed. Two cars have collided and a mysterious black mist has attacked one of them, flaying its occupants alive, before being sucked into the body of the driver of the other car. He's Evan Michaels and he's our protagonist. Now, if that might suggest that he's some sort of monster or villain, I should correct you on that immediately, as he's merely the unwilling carrier of the black mist, which is the Rider of the title, and he's as horrified as we are at what happened, even though the sensation that he feels as it returns to his body is literally described as orgasmic.

In a typical horror novel, this Rider would be the only Rider and we'd spend the next couple of hundred pages learning about what sort of supernatural being it is and why it's hitched an unwelcome ride in Evan's body, all while it wreaks its havoc across the countryside. Of course, eventually, he'd figure out how to destroy it and all would be right with the world again, at least until another one shows up on the last page and we wait a year or so for the inevitable sequel. However, Moe is not interested in writing a typical horror novel, so what we get here is a combination of dark fantasy, thriller and, oddly, romance.

The romance angle literally pulls up in front of Evan as he leaves the scene of this inexplicable atrocity and climbs out in "a swirl of long skirts and auburn ringlets". It's Cerise Metuchen, she took a whole lot of classes with him in school and her presence here at the side of a highway at night is not accidental in the slightest. Sure, Moe happily milks it as convenience for most of a chapter but it soon becomes clear that Cerise and her companion, Miz V, know exactly what happened, as well as potentially why, and they can do something about it, which is massively important because the carriers of Riders in this world will not be allowed to wander around letting the black mist inside them commit mass murder whenever they feel like it; they're executed on live television instead.

The good news is that we soon learn a lot more about Riders and witches, as that's what Cerise and Miz V are, and it's easily enough to ground us in what's going on in this version of Arizona. It's recognisable as our state, right down to the presence of In-N-Out Burger, but it isn't our state because certain things are very different; I guess we could call it a sort of parallel universe version. The bad news is that we never learn enough, probably due to Moe leaving that for the sequel that we haven't seen yet. The core story is certainly resolved here, so I don't mean to complain, but I'm eager to learn more and yet I ran out of pages.

The dark fantasy angle stems mostly from the setup. Riders exist and they appear out of nowhere, glom onto poor souls who wouldn't say boo to a goose and then use them as a combination of accommodation and transport, unwilling vessels to carry them around on murder sprees. This is not information that's known only to us, by the way. Everyone knows it and there's even a police department, inevitably called the Rider Division, to counter it. As this murderous mist is seen, rather understandably, as bad, it falls to this department to catch the hosts and the state to execute them.

However, witches also exist, in an organised fashion, in an ancient and well-known Order that feels much more like a convent than a coven. There is a Roman Catholic church in this world, because the Order has succeeded it in levels of importance. However, the two are familiar in many ways. Instead of a Vatican, a Pope and a male priesthood, there's a Citadel, an Abbess and female acolytes, all based at Marcella Peak in Phoenix. That's some quick growth, given that it grew out of a notorious Purge of witches and was officially founded as recently as 1842. However, there is a lineage to it that goes all the way back to Biblical times that I won't spoil.

So far, so good. The catch to this, if we consider it so, is in how these witches are able to mitigate Riders, which start to feel rather like demons. They use ritual, which we might expect, and it's sexual ritual, which feels like wish fulfilment. So you're a young man and you suddenly find that a Rider has attached itself to you, meaning that you now have a target on your back because your country has every intention of executing you. But blink, and there's a gorgeous young witch ready to help you by using her powers of ritualistic sex.

Maybe this isn't dark fantasy, it's just goth girl fantasy. Don't forget that all those acolytes at the Citadel need to be trained in ritual sex and someone's going to have to take that job. Does my resume need updating? I wonder why I thought of that, all of a sudden.

The thriller angle, of course, is partly in the chase that quickly ensues. However, there are other levels to consider. For one, the lead cop from the Rider Division hunting Evan is Nicole Davis, a former witch with a history with the Order. She's definitely good at her job and that background means that she knows more than her peers, both of which help to ratchet up the tension. However, the book isn't ever going to be just a chase, as there's so much more going on, with a succession battle unfolding at the Citadel, secret operations that we learn about only gradually and an unprecedented number of Riders manifesting in Phoenix with the goal of killing the Abbess.

The romance angle shows up with Evan and Cerise, of course, and it's almost shockingly welcome. Maybe it's a way to mitigate the sex thing, by shifting it sideways into romance. Maybe it's a way to mitigate the evil thing too, given that Evan was part of a double homicide on the very first page and yet we're supposed to sympathise with his plight. So yeah, he's a young man who paints book covers for a living and falls in love with the witch who's trying to save him, who falls in love with him too. Oh yeah, but they're still fugitives from the law and that means they should probably get out of bed at some point real soon now.

I wonder if the reason why we haven't seen the promised sequel yet, *Rider: Unity*, is due to Moe having a hard task on his hands figuring out exactly what he wrote here. In many ways, this is a YA novel with sex, thus something that doesn't precisely fit anywhere. As dark fantasy, it holds back. The mythology here is fascinating, but it's never as visceral as it was on the first page. As a thriller, it holds back as well, due to the fantasy always being more important and so leaving the focus rarely on the chase. Even when it does, it's always far more about the chased than the chaser. As a romance, it's sweet and YA, but it has a sexual component that would be out of place there, even though it's never lurid and exploitative.

If Moe ditched the sex, this would be a solid YA read. Leaving it in means that everything's tamer than it ought to be. And, given that it's done and dusted and *Rider* has been in print for a decade, how should he approach the sequel? Inquiring minds want to know.

MEGAN E. VAUGHN

THE EMERALD DOOR

PUBLISHER:
FIVE SMILING FISH

PUBLICATION DATE:
MAY 2015

Boy, was this one fun! No, it's not the best novel I've read this year and it's not the heaviest either, but it has a pretty good shot at winning out as the most fun. I devoured it in a single sitting and found myself with a grin on my face for a good chunk of it. However, it's far from challenging, even as a YA read, and it has a sort of interactive mindset where we guess at what's going to be waiting for Dory on the next floor of her new apartment building. But I'm getting ahead of myself. Let's back up.

Dory is a lonely young lady who keeps to herself, which is simple to do in the Kansas Heights apartment block, because everyone does that. But a storm blows in and the block blows out, so she's forced to move, her father snagging a first floor apartment in the Optical Zenith building. If you're paying attention to those details, you'll see a common theme developing already and it's very deliberate. Dory is short for Dorothea, or Dorothy, and, well, she's not in Kansas anymore. She's in OZ. And, just as *The Wizard of Oz* is a fantasy that takes place within a fantasy, there's a picture book in the wreckage that neatly telegraphs what Dory is going to see, including a vampire, a werewolf and a ghost.

The Wizard of Oz was a children's book, of course, before it became a whole slew of movies, and this is a children's story too, even if it's dressed up for Hallowe'en. I'd love to have read this at five, but I have no complaints reading it at fifty and change. Sure, it's light. Sure, Dory takes everything that happens in a childlike fashion, accepting things immediately for what they are and moving right along, as if it's usual to deal with the supernatural on a constant basis. Sure, it's easy to see how a different filter could have been applied to the entire book and every scene in it to turn it into an adult horror novel. But that's not what Megan Vaughn had in mind and that's fine.

I liked how everything was just a little off once Dory gets to OZ. This isn't a picture book, so Vaughn had no way of shifting from sepia to TechniColor, but she makes a shift in tone to mimic that. The first person Dory meets in OZ is "boringly handsome" like a model, but also sick and obviously so. And, of course, he's far from the last strange character she will meet as she makes her way upstairs. Right after moving in, she discovers that the three month lease that she signed says three years on it. She needs to talk to the landlord to square it away, but he lives on the tenth floor, behind the Emerald Door of the title. What's more, he has no phone and he only communicates through a newsletter. So, up the stairs she goes.

What's waiting on the second floor is a crazy cat lady who provides her with some important back story. The previous tenant of Dory's room was a hermit who died there after fifty years of residency. And her sister, up on thirteen, wants something of hers. No prizes for guessing that what she wants is what Dory found there on her first day, but it's good to have a MacGuffin.

What's waiting on the third floor is the scarecrow. OK, he's really a ghost with a shock of straw-coloured hair, but I doubt anyone will fail to acknowledge that he's the scarecrow at this point. We're in Oz and we're off to see the wizard. Of course, once we're past the witch, we're going to meet the scarecrow. He's called Ghost and he's amnesiac, so wants his memory

back; he also wants to figure out how to scare people as he's really not very good at that.

Similarly, the vampire on four is Raleigh who has no empathy and wants to be able to feel again, while the werewolf on five is Winston, who's scared of almost everything, an agoraphobic and claustrophobic mess. No brain, no heart, no courage. Scarecrow, tin man, cowardly lion. Did I mention that Dory has a little dog too, called Frank? Did I tell you what colour her sneakers are? Hey, you know already. I can tell that you're following nicely.

And, as transparent a translation of *The Wizard of Oz* into a mildly spooky apartment block as this is, I was absolutely following too, as Dory climbs each flight of stairs on her way to the Emerald Door on the tenth floor. Hey, I'm a poet and I don't know it! And that may be the only thing she doesn't meet on her way. Well, their way, because you won't be shocked to discover that Ghost, Raleigh and Winston join her on her quest, because they have their own reasons to talk to the landlord and there's safety in numbers.

As you can imagine, there are precious few surprises here. We all know the story because we've read it and we've watched it and probably more than once in both cases. What Vaughn does to counter that is to make this highly episodic, with each floor of the OZ building offering a fresh shock and a fresh solution. I liked how she made sure that it wasn't just Dory's show, by being even-handed with these characters. Everyone is involved in conversation. Everyone gets opportunity to look both good and bad. Everyone develops as a character, even if that development is inevitably rather predictable.

What isn't predictable is what's waiting on the next floor because, while everything is so episodic that this novel could have been twice the length just by doubling the height of the building, Vaughn doesn't go for cliffhangers to set us up for the next chapter. Maybe there were a couple here and there, but it's not a routine approach, so we find ourselves climbing the stairs with our colourful party, knowing that something's going to be up there but knowing too that it's not just going to jump out to scare us. This is a YA fantasy, remember, not an adult horror novel.

And, as little as the progression of monsters really matters in the grand scheme of things, I'll leave you to experience them with Dory and her crew. I'll just mention that they're all fun in their way, they each add to the lessons learned and they run through the majority of monsters you're going to imagine will show up at some point. Yes, there's a giant spider. Of course, there's a giant spider. There are also... nah, you won't trick me into telling you. Buy the book and read it for yourself. Or read it aloud to the kids in your life. They'll have fun with it and so will you.

Given that we know that the Wizard of Oz isn't at all what he pretended to be, we can safely assume that there are some shenanigans planned for when our heroes make it all the way to the tenth floor, the Emerald Door, and Vaughn does her job when we get to that point. The quest changes a little and, if you were paying attention early on, you'll likely have guessed exactly how it changes already. But this isn't a book to read for surprises, it's a book to read for comfort. It's an old favourite that you simply haven't read yet.

If you're old and curmudgeonly like me, this is going to seem a little light. I don't know what age group this was written for, but it's an age group that's a heck of a lot younger than

me. My eighteen-year old granddaughter may get a kick out of this, but it's going to seem a little light to her too. Maybe the fourteen-year-old is the right age. Maybe it would be better sitting on a shelf, waiting for the eight-year-old to reach double digits. And, as I mentioned, it feels like it would be a great book to read aloud, even without pictures to bolster the experience.

Certainly the biggest downside to the book would vanish if it's read aloud, because there are a number of typos here that won't show up that way. They're the sort of typos that show up when you spellcheck a book diligently but don't proof it particularly well. You only have to wait until page nine to track down a couple: "stared" for "started" and "deigned" instead of "designed". Both words are real words, just not the right words. And so it goes, with "dating sights", "scrapped fingertips" and a "forth pumpkin". I could add that the entire book is laid out in a sans-serif font, which is a little jarring, but that's fair for the audience, I think.

Quite frankly, if those are the biggest problems with the book, they're pretty minor and not difficult to fix in a second edition. And it has to be said that they are hardly unusual problems for small press publications. At least this has justified text with good margins. I've seen a heck of a lot worse. And I'm hardly immune either. Just look at the spine on my second book. I'm still tempted to put out a second edition just to change that to something readable. And, if I did, I could also fix... yeah, that way lies utter madness. Just like the thirteenth floor.

When your life is a reality show, falling in love with your best friend is a game changer.

SARA FUJIMURA

FAKING REALITY

PUBLISHER:
TOR TEEN

PUBLICATION DATE:
JULY 2022

It's fair to say that this has to be the single most unlikely of the six hundred or so books I've reviewed at the Nameless Zine thus far. I enjoy a lot of different genres of fiction but YA romance really isn't on the list and factoring in the important reality TV angle moves it even further away from being something I might like. However, I know Sara Fujimura. I've shared a table at Phoenix Comicon with her, back when she was promoting her self-published debut novel, *Tanabata Wish*. This one says Tor Teen on the spine because the awards she won for that book and its follow-up, *Every Reason We Shouldn't*, clearly raised awareness of her talent and she was snapped up by a major. I could not be happier to see a local author make it big and therefore I had to

check this one out.

What surprised me isn't that it's a decent book, because, of course, it is. What surprised me is how much I enjoyed it, being so far outside of my comfort zone, and that's mostly due to two very clear reasons.

Firstly, I didn't dislike anyone—not the lead character, Dakota McDonald; not Leo Matsuda, her best friend for almost her entire life, who is shocked when she tries to kiss him and relegates her firmly into the friend zone; and not even the eventual third wheels who complicate matters, one of those for each of them. The reason I'm not a romance fan isn't just because they're kissing books shorn of all the swashbuckling adventure they could have had, but because I tend to dislike the characters, both male and female. I've always found them selfish, picky and discardable, which are the absolute last words any romance writer wants readers to associate with characters that they are supposed to either identify with or ache for with passion.

Now, of course I didn't identify with any of these characters because I'm a grandfather and they're all teenagers, and I didn't ache for Koty McDonald, which is good because that would have been weird. However, I felt like she was eminently worthy as a character, as someone struggling to remain grounded given a celebrity life that she never asked for, and someone whose feelings for her best friend simply grew as she did. It can't remotely be a spoiler to point out that she ends up with Leo and I was happy for her, even if it took him far too long to wake up and smell the cinnamon rolls. OK, maybe I identified with him just a little on that front. My neurodivergent brain simply doesn't process flirting when it's done to me, so I'm very good indeed at oblivious.

Secondly, while the book exists to get Koty and Leo together at the end, Fujimura builds their world in a far more substantial manner than I ever expected from a YA romance. They each have lives of their own and both of those lives come with responsibilities. Koty's is more obvious because she's on television, a blessing and a curse, but the responsibilities she has to her parents and the show they present on HGTV are really no different from the responsibilities that Leo has to his family and their Japanese restaurant. In both instances, they do what they need to do, but they also try to find a way to find what we might fairly call a work/life balance, which is an even more awkward concept for them because they're both still in school.

For Koty, she was literally born into stardom. Her parents, both forty-six at the time and four years into presenting a DIY show called *If These Walls Could Talk*, didn't expect to have a daughter, but she showed up anyway and thus literally grew up on television. That's great for the trust fund, of course, but not so good when her embarrassment at a homecoming dance is spoofed on *Saturday Night Live*. Leo isn't famous at all, but he grew up doing whatever needed to be done at Matsuda, his family's restaurant, both to keep it open and serving up food. Both appreciate their work but also want to escape it, so they can figure out who they are away from the lives that they were born into.

And it seems pretty obvious from moment one that they'll be doing that together. Koty practically lives at Matsuda, helping out even when it's not Monday when her family dines there like clockwork. She and Leo share a love of Japanese culture, Leo being Japanese American and Koty a quarter Japanese. They enjoy a TV show together called *Kitsune Mask*, listen to J-pop and study the Japanese language. They are even planning to visit Japan together, as part of a trip organised by their school's Japanese Culture Club. It's hard to imagine one without the other, which, of course, is where we kinda-sorta end up when Koty expresses a deeper level of feeling and Leo rebuffs her.

And so we focus on the details, while Koty and Leo either avoid each other or hang out together with a little awkwardness taking the sheen off the good and simple times that they would otherwise be. And that's exactly where Fujimura's worldbuilding works so well. I'm sure that romance fans never like the scenes where clearly destined couples completely fail to live up to their promise but they're always necessary. After all, how is a couple supposed to get back together if they're not apart to begin with? The middle chunk of the book with Leo dating Lindsay and Koty dating Alex could easily have been an utter waste of space because we know deep inside our soul that neither of those relationships is going to work. What saves it is all that worldbuilding detail.

We never get to see *If These Walls Could Talk*, of course, and, having not watched *Fixer Upper*, its real life influence, I'm still not entirely sure how it would play, but we get to see behind the scenes and that worked for me. I liked the details that firm up how different a life Koty has being on this show to the rest of us, like how that life is four months adrift because of the time between shooting an episode and its eventual air date, meaning that they celebrate Thanksgiving in August and Christmas in September, to remain "current" on air.

We also don't get to eat at Matsuda, though I guarantee that every reader, whether they get invested in the romance or not, will want to work through their entire menu, but we similarly get to see behind those scenes and that worked for me too. There's a lot less adjustment needed and a lot more good old fashioned hard work, but I appreciated learning about how a restaurant functions just as much as I did how a DIY show functions. In many ways, the romance—or indeed the lack of it as these kids figure things out—was a minor angle for me, even if it would be the primary one for most readers.

I also liked some of the ground that Fujimura covers here. Not only are both leads at least partly of another race, without the book ever getting preachy at all, but there's also an immersion into Japanese culture and cuisine that never gets gimmicky. It's all thoroughly

grounded and told very believably. Knowing a little of Sara's background, having met some of her family, I can understand where that came from but it's still impressive that she could get so much of that down onto the page in such a grounded way. There's also a genderfluid friend for Koty and Leo in Neviah, whose pronouns we learn but who also never becomes preachy or gimmicky, even if their inclusion has to be underpinning for the core theme of self-identity. That's clever writing.

And so I enjoyed this a lot more than I expected and for reasons I didn't expect to manifest. Next time I see a book with a pink cover and a title in whatever light shade of teal that counts as, that details the eventual romance between a pair of teenagers, I should read that too. Nah, maybe not. But I am happy that I picked this one up. It's a lot more than just a local author making good.

SUBMISSIONS

I welcome submissions to Apocalypse Later Music, though I can't guarantee that everything submitted will be reviewed.

Please read the following important notes before submitting anything.

I primarily review the good stuff. There's just too much of it out there nowadays to waste any time reviewing the bad stuff. Almost everything that I review is, in my opinion, either good or interesting and, hopefully, both. I believe that it's worth listening to and I recommend it to some degree, if it happens to be your sort of thing. Now, if you're a die hard black/death metalhead, you might not dig any of the psychedelic rock and vice versa. However, maybe you will! Open ears, open minds and all that.

I have zero interest in being a hatchet man critic who slams everything he writes about. I'll only give a bad review if it's in the public interest, such as a major act releasing a disappointing album. Even then, I'll often keep away.

If I do review, I'll still be completely honest and point out the good and the bad in any release.

I'm primarily reviewing new material only. Each month at Apocalypse Later Music, I review releases from the previous two months. I might stretch a little beyond that for a submission, but not far. Each January, I also try to catch up with highly regarded albums and obvious omissions from the previous year that I didn't get round to at the time. I then bundle my reviews up at the end of a quarter and publish in zine form midway through the following month.

I'm especially interested in studio albums or EPs that do something new and different. I try to review an indie release and a major band each weekday, one rock and one metal, with each week deliberately varied in both genres and countries covered.

If you still want to submit, thank you! You can do so in a couple of ways:

1. Digital copy: please e-mail me at hal@hornsablaze.com a link to where I can download mp3s in 320k. Please include promotional material such as an EPK, high res cover art, etc.
2. Physical: e-mail me for a mailing address.

Either way but especially digitally, please include any promotional material such as a press kit, high res cover art, band photo, etc.

And, whether you submit or not and whether I liked it or not, all the best with your music! Don't quit! The world is a better place because you create.

Submissions of books for review at the Nameless Zine wouldn't come to me directly. If you have books that fit the scope of a predominantly science fiction/fantasy/horror e-zine, please see the contact details at the bottom of the main page at thenamelesszine.org.

I don't review film submissions much any more, as most of my film reviews are for books.

CREATIVE COMMONS

This *Library of Halexandria* zine, like the books published by Apocalypse Later Press and the reviews posted to Apocalypse Later Reviews, whether books, films or music, is licensed through Creative Commons, using the CC BY-NC-SA 3.0 copyleft license.

This means that anyone is legally allowed to copy and distribute, as long as they:

1. Clearly identify the author of the work (BY). That's me, Hal C. F. Astell.
2. Do so on a non-commercial basis (NC). That means you don't make money doing it.
3. Do not change the terms of this licence (SA).

So please download this zine for free at press.apocalypselaterempire.com and read it, print it, copy it, translate it and otherwise share it so it and the bands covered within it can reach as wide an audience as is possible. Piracy is not the enemy. Obscurity is the enemy. Horns ablaze!

Of course, you can just buy a copy from Amazon instead and that would be appreciated too. That helps pay the bills and keep this zine happening.

Also, all album or book covers, band or author photos, film posters and screenshots remain copyrighted to their respective creators, photographers or owners.

ABOUT HAL C. F. ASTELL

While he still has a day job to pay the bills, Hal C. F. Astell is a teacher by blood and a writer by the grace of the Dread Lord, which gradually transformed him into a film critic. He primarily writes for his own site, Apocalypse Later, but also anyone else who asks nicely. He writes monthly book reviews for the Nameless Zine.

Born and raised in the cold and rain of England half a century ago, he's still learning about the word "heat" many years after moving to Phoenix, Arizona where he lives with his much better half Dee in a house full of critters and oddities, a library with a ghost guard ferret and more cultural artefacts than can comfortably be imagined. And he can imagine quite a lot.

Just in case you care, his favourite film is Peter Jackson's debut, *Bad Taste*; his favourite actor is Warren William; and he believes Carl Theodor Dreyer's *The Passion of Joan of Arc* is the greatest movie ever made.

He reads science fiction, horror and the pulps. He watches anything unusual and much that isn't. He listens to everything except mainstream western pop music. He annoys those around him by talking too much about Guy N. Smith, Doc Savage and the *Friday Rock Show*.

He tries not to go outdoors, but he's usually easy to find at film festivals, conventions and events because he's likely to be the only one there in kilt and forked beard, while his fading English accent is instantly recognisable on podcasts and panels. He hasn't been trepanned yet, but he's friendly and doesn't bite unless asked.

Photo Credit: Dee Astell

My personal site is Dawtrina. I run Smithland, a Guy N. Smith fan site. I founded and co-run the CoKoCon science fiction/fantasy convention. I co-founded the Arizona Penny Dreadfuls. I've run the Awesomelys since 2013. I write for the Nameless Zine.

The Arizona Penny Dreadfuls	azpennydreadfuls.org
The Awesomelys	awesomelys.com
CoKoCon	cokocon.org
Dawtrina	dawtrina.com
The Nameless Zine	thenamelesszine.org
Smithland	guynsmith.rocks

ABOUT APOCALYPSE LATER

Initially, Hal C. F. Astell wrote film reviews for his own reference as he could never remember who the one good actor was in forgettable episodes of long crime film series from the forties. After a year, they became long enough to warrant a dedicated blog.

The name came from an abandoned project in which he was reviewing his way through every movie in the IMDb Top 250 list. Its tentative title was a joke drawn from covering *Apocalypse Now* last and it stuck. It didn't have to be funny.

Gradually he focused on writing at length about the sort of films that most critics don't, such as old films, foreign films, indie films, local films, microbudget films, and so on, always avoiding adverts, syndication and monetised links, not to forget the eye-killing horror of white text on a black background. Let's just get to the content and make it readable.

Four million words later and Apocalypse Later Press was born, in order to publish his first book, cunningly titled *Huh?* It's been followed by half a dozen others with double digits more always in process.

This growth eventually turned into the Apocalypse Later Empire, which continues to sprawl. In addition to film and book reviews, he posts a pair of album reviews each weekday from across the rock/metal spectrum and around the globe. He runs the only dedicated annual genre film festival in Phoenix, Arizona, the Apocalypse Later International Fantastic Film Festival, or ALIFFF. He publishes books by himself and others. He presents programs of quality international short films at conventions across the southwest.

Apocalypse Later is celebrating its fifteenth anniversary in 2022.

Apocalypse Later Empire	apocalypselaterempire.com
Apocalypse Later Film	apocalypselaterfilm.com
Apocalypse Later Books	books.apocalypselaterempire.com
Apocalypse Later Music	apocalypselatermusic.com
Apocalypse Later International Fantastic Film Festival	alfilmfest.com
Apocalypse Later Roadshow	roadshow.apocalypselaterempire.com
Apocalypse Later Press	press.apocalypselaterempire.com
Apocalypse Later Now!	apocalypselaternow.blogspot.com
Horns Ablaze	hornsablaze.com

Latest Books from Apocalypse Later Press (available on Amazon):

The Awesomely Awful '80s, Part 2
A Horror Movie Calendar

SCIENCE FICTION & FANTASY CONVENTION

Seanan McGuire
Author Guest of Honor
COKOCON

andyvanoverberghe
Artist Guest of Honor
COKOCON

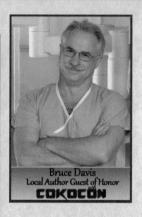

Bruce Davis
Local Author Guest of Honor
COKOCON

Bruce Davis and andyvanoverberghe sponsored by Arizona Fandom
Margaret & Kristoph sponsored by the Phoenix Filk Circle
Gilead sponsored in part by T.G. Geeks

Margaret Davis
Filk Guest of Honor
COKOCON

Gilead
Artist In Residence
COKOCON

Kristoph Klover
Filk Guest of Honor
COKOCON

COKOCON.ORG

Made in the USA
Columbia, SC
29 October 2024